Imagery for Preaching

FORTRESS RESOURCES FOR PREACHING

Robert G. Hughes, *A Trumpet in Darkness*
Donald Macleod, *The Problem of Preaching*
John Mason Stapleton, *Preaching in Demonstration
of the Spirit and Power*
David G. Buttrick, *Preaching Jesus Christ*
Sheldon A. Tostengard, *The Spoken Word*
Richard L. Thulin, *The "I" of the Sermon*

IMAGERY FOR PREACHING

PATRICIA WILSON-KASTNER

FORTRESS PRESS   MINNEAPOLIS

Library of Congress Cataloging-in-Publication Data

Wilson-Kastner, Patricia, 1944–
    Imagery for preaching / Patricia Wilson-Kastner.
       p.   cm.—(Fortress resources for preaching)
    Bibliography: p.
    ISBN 0–8006–1150–0
    1. Preaching. 2. Figures of speech. I. Title. II. Series.
BV4226.W55   1989
251—dc20   89–34196
                                                    CIP

Printed in the United States of America   1–1150

To the Rev. Rachel Hosmer, O.S.H.,
whose compassionate wisdom has illumined our lives
so that God's own Spirit may fill the depth of our hearts

Contents

Acknowledgments

The major themes of this book began to percolate during a summer class in preaching I taught at the invitation of Dr. William Phillips of Vancouver School of Theology in 1986. That summer I also offered a series of lectures about imagery and the Bible at a conference entitled "Creation Around the Chesapeake" in St. Mary's City, Maryland, sponsored by the Episcopal Diocese of Washington, D.C., and St. Mary's Parish. Some of the ideas in chapters 1 and 5 were originally presented in April 1987 as the Wertsch Lectures at the St. Paul School of Theology in Kansas City, Missouri. Dr. Eugene Lowrie of the St. Paul faculty responded to those presentations with great encouragement and help. Some of the material in chapters 2 and 3 was presented in different form in lectures that Dr. David Schlafer had invited me to deliver in March 1987 at Nashota House in Wisconsin. Students in classes over the last six years at the General Theological Seminary in New York City have contributed criticism and encouragement.

The dean, faculty, and trustees of the General Theological Seminary enabled me to take a sabbatical and study leave during 1986–87. The Conant Foundation provided financial resources that allowed me to explore some of the connections among parish life, preaching, and theology as lived out in two Manhattan Episcopal parishes—St. Mark's in the Bowery and Christ and St. Stephen. Much collegial support was supplied by the Revs. David Garcia, Beatrice Blair, Joseph Zorawick, Charles Haskins, and Raymond Messler.

Many kind friends and colleagues have been gracious enough to read and comment on all or part of the manuscript. I thank especially Dr. Arthur van Seters; Bishop John Coburn; the Rev. Rachel Hosmer, O.S.H.; and the Rev. Paul Wessinger, S.S.J.E. Dr. John A. Hollar, Senior Editor for Fortress Press, has offered his customary cogent, thorough, and compelling observations, all the while encouraging me. Alice Madden has patiently and capably typed the manuscript through many different redactions.

Without the constant enthusiasm and support of my spouse, G. Ronald Kastner, who has patiently listened to innumerable sermons over the years, and commented on the text of my book with faithful and intelligent criticism, I could never have completed this work.

Patricia Wilson-Kastner
Trinity Church Professor of Preaching
All Saints' Day, 1988

Introduction

Today one of the most complex challenges is to keep people interested in a sermon. Throughout history, of course, the boring preacher has been a stock-in-trade comedy character. But today's preacher is acutely aware that the bored parishioner will not suffer in silence. A consistently boring preacher will produce a congregation reduced in numbers, as well as in spiritual health. People who find a preacher's sermons tedious turn the preacher off and sometimes leave the church.

In the thirteenth century, the Dominican Humbert of Romans could unapologetically write to encourage budding preachers that preaching was a complex and difficult, but noble, task because Jesus appointed the apostles to preach, angels are called preachers of salvation, and God became incarnate to preach to human beings.

> "Now the apostles are the most outstanding of all the saints, angels are the most outstanding of all the creatures, and in all that exists, nothing is more outstanding than God. So a job which is apostolic, angelic, and divine must be outstanding!"[1]

Contemporary preachers would be far less certain of the exalted status of their own preaching, but would certainly agree with Humbert: Preaching is an outstanding task, with problems enough even for God incarnate.

One can try to produce religious spectaculars, with musical extravaganzas and blood-curdling or emotionally draining sermons. Unhappily, these approaches tend to offer a cheap gospel and cheap grace. They also have little effect on people's lives. They play to surface thoughts and feelings and soon evaporate.

Our preaching does not have to move between theologically sound boredom and flashy, shallow, religious hype. Contemporary science and theology, as well as the Scriptures themselves, offer us a more solid and humanly effective approach to preaching. Today more attention than ever before is being paid to the importance of imagery and the sensory-affective dimension of the human person. Anthropologists, biologists, poets, and theologians are all trying to understand this aspect of humans, long neglected by Western civilization.

As we are growing in our appreciation of the complexity of the human person, we are recognizing that we need to learn more about how we can effectively communicate with the whole human person. In this discussion, interest in narrative- and image-centered preaching has arisen and flourished.

Narrative-centered preaching centers on a fundamental biblical reality: God's self-revelation is not given to us through the abstract propositions of systematic theology, but through the story of God's relationship with human beings in their history. All theology is reflection on this story and our participation in it. Therefore, effective preaching is narrative preaching (storytelling) sharing in the medium and the message of biblical revelation. Narrative preaching of course concerns itself primarily with plot—the sequence of events as arranged by the author—and characters, motivations, and conflicts.[2]

Biblical revelation and effective preaching, however, encompass not only plot and motivation but also the whole sensory dimension of the human characters and the world in which we live. The sensory dimension of the Scriptures, in which God's self-revelation to us is expressed, is encompassed in the term "imagery."[3] Imagery includes pictures and images, such as "God is my rock," but also includes the sensory qualities of individuals and groups, the physical environment, comparisons, metaphors, and similes. Imagery is another dimension of the world of specific persons and events in which our faith is revealed to us.

As we all know, our contemporary world presses us to take seriously the importance of imagery to us and to our mental processes. In Western culture, we have for centuries considered material reality—the specific and concrete—to be inferior to the intellectual or spiritual realm. The best we could do for embodied reality would be for our minds to make concrete beings into abstract propositions or scientific hypotheses. Today we are rediscovering the integrity and the significance of the physical stuff of ordinary life. We are much more aware that our contact, with ourselves and the world around us, depends more on the senses and sensory reality than the abstractions we have so often regarded as truth.

Of particular importance to preachers is the growing recognition that verbal, abstract expression is the province of a few, whereas the visual, sensory, and imagery filled discourse is accessible to virtually everyone.[4] The simple reality is that the preaching most accessible to most people in the congregation is based on imagery and attention to the physical. This fact does not mean that preaching is only about the physical world or is confined to what we see and hear. But effective preaching is rooted and focused in the physical and sensory. Abstract, proposition-centered preaching affects few people and tends not to reach people at their spiritual and psychological depths. Most humans are not, as we will see, constituted to thrive on abstractions.

Preaching cannot be true to itself if it is a series of abstractions or a string of exhortations, because most fundamentally, preaching is prayer. Christian liturgical preaching is an integral part of the community's prayer to God, in which we receive from God and give with thanks. Preaching is that part of liturgical prayer in which the preacher, for the community, proclaims before God our remembrance of God's saving acts in the past, our awareness of divine presence here and now, and our response to God in our lives. Preaching is the prayer that specifically connects this community's past, present, and future to God. In this respect, it shares a common characteristic with all prayer which is dialogue between God and humanity. In *The Christ We Know*, John Booty refers to a passage in *Ecclesiastical Polity* in which Hooker compares corporate prayer to the ascending and descending angels of Jacob's vision.[5] The ascending and descending angels remind us of prayer's peculiar quality of addressing heaven and earth.

Our corporate worship is not just a gathering of like-minded people to share inspiring messages or exhortations to noble action. Liturgy is community prayer, in which together we restore our individual and corporate selves in contact with God. To remember liturgically the Jesus who died, was buried, and rose again is to be joined and to join ourselves to the living Christ through the power of the Holy Spirit. Preaching in the worshiping community expresses God's grace to us and our response to God. It is not primarily teaching or exhortation; preaching is prayer.

Liturgical, corporate prayer is the prayer of the embodied world, humanity with its hands and feet and voices, praising God and listening to God's self-revelation in the world. This book explores some of the connections between our human existence as embodied persons, encompassing physical and mental dimensions, with preaching as an aspect of liturgical prayer. In this process we will explore some recent developments in our culture's renewed awareness of physical reality, and ask about the importance of the physical in the biblical world view through examining images and imagery in Old and New Testaments. After inquiring about what imagery in sermons is and does, we will look at a style of prayer that is particularly constructive in preparing sermons. We will consider a sermon that emerges from this prayer and inquire into how such preaching contributes to the whole liturgy. From the beginning we will proceed with this vision of the relationship between preaching and corporate prayer. Rooted in the liturgy, preaching shares in its visible, tangible, sensory character. As the grace-filled interchange between God and humanity is focused in the sacramental character of the liturgy, so preaching expresses the connection between God's revealing word in Scripture and human reception and response.

Much of the contemporary theory of preaching expresses elements of this vision. It is vitally concerned that preaching show to others the activity of God among us, inviting us also to share in God's action among us.[6] If we want to do this work in the church at all, presumably we want to do it as effectively as possible. A key to effectiveness is the very nature of preaching itself: *Preaching is an address to the worshiping community as a part of the liturgy, and thus is part of the church's prayer to God.* A sermon shows, explores, and explains God's grace and our response to God in order to draw the community closer to God and to one another—in all aspects of their lives.

In the past preaching has often been physically and psychologically detached from the rest of the liturgy. Frequently it has been reduced to either moral exhortation or dogmatic instruction. Contemporary developments in our understanding of human nature and the integrity of a humanity that is affective and cognitive, physical and spiritual, press us to acknowledge that if we would be heard, then our preaching must address the whole human being. If we would be effective preachers, we need to develop our own awareness of imagery as well as express it in our sermons.

In this effort to be effective preachers, three fundamental insights emerging from contemporary thought are essential to an image-centered approach to preaching:

1. Today as we reflect on our culture, we are increasingly aware that neither the rational/logical nor the intuitive/affective interpretation of

reality is superior to the other, or is alone adequate to explain reality. Each is essential to us, individually and corporately. *We do in fact think with images.* For most of us, "thought" is a complex activity encompassing reasoning, intuiting, and feeling. The focus for that activity is almost always in the sensory realm. We express and explain ourselves in more complex and holistic ways.

2. As members of creation, human beings are part of a complex, multidimensional, interrelated whole. The world is both tactile and spiritual, accessible to us in varied ways. Because of the varied aspects of our world, we must relate to it in diverse ways—some more abstract, others more concrete, some more distant, others more close, some by image, and some by concept. *Today we are rediscovering the necessity of images, imagination, and feeling.* Today we are acknowledging that if we wish to more fully know and experience ourselves and our world, as well as the God who acts among us, the image-centered, the intuitive, and the imaginative visions are central to preaching.

3. We are increasingly aware that *imagery is multidimensional.* Images are concrete referents, with intellectual, cognitive elements and affective aspects. Imagery—of rock, tree, or sun, for instance—allows us to connect God with our world and with ourselves, because these concrete objects are part of our experience while also pointing beyond themselves. At the same time that we perceive in the image of the rock aspects of ourselves and of the natural world that supports us and offers us security, we also perceive a dimension of the holy and transcendent that is present in rock, together with a stability surpassing any humanly experienced rock. The image of the rock allows all those elements to be present and held together in one concrete reality.

4. Today we are learning better how to allow these images to open to us the richness of the interrelationship between the divine and the human, ourselves and the rest of creation. *One piece of reality—an image—can focus all of reality in itself for us.* We can and must learn to preach in such a mode because it is a more faithful and effective address to the fullness of our humanity.

If we preach with more attention to whole human beings and their mental processes, then we will discover that our sermons help open up people's feelings as well as thoughts and intentions to the religious dimension of life. Our sermons will assist people to integrate their thoughts and feelings in one focused perception of reality and to respond in a more humanly comprehensive way to God's self-revelation. Our sermons may also help people open their emotions and the physical aspects of their lives to God's grace in a thoughtful, disciplined, and generous way, because they will feel more of God's activity in the whole of their lives.

A more comprehensive, deliberate, and thorough use of imagery in preaching is not a quick fix to make us more popular preachers, or even to help us compose our sermons more quickly. The approach suggested here offers no short cuts. If practiced with faithfulness, hard work, and openness to God's Spirit active in our lives, this may help us preach more effectively and more prayerfully. Such imagistic preaching may draw us closer together in the richness of God's grace, which has been given to us in all wisdom and insight. I hope this book will offer a new beginning point for us as we explore new visions of human consciousness, and offer us insights into more effective expression—in new and old ways.

1
Imagery
and the Mind

Every preacher knows how important good images and word pictures are to engage her congregation with the sermon. Effective sermons have always attempted to embody the truth, expressing in words the physical texture and quality of the world that God created and in which the Word becomes flesh. But within the last twenty years or so our understanding of human consciousness has expanded, and we have become increasingly conscious of the centrality of the concrete, the affective, the specific, and the imaginative. Images are not just a gimmick to attract people before giving them solid doctrine. Images are not candy, while abstractions are meat. Today's preacher lives in a world that is steadily moving in its appraisal of human nature toward a balance of the intellectual and the emotional, the rational and the intuitive.

If preachers hope to communicate effectively with congregations, then we ignore this new emphasis on images and imagery at our peril. Such a convergence of conviction by theologians, philosophers, psychologists, biologists, anthropologists, educators, and others alerts us to a new awareness of the interrelationship of body and psyche, abstract and concrete, intellect and imagination.

IMAGERY: A KEY TO OUR UNIVERSE

Today we are experiencing a revolution in our understanding of human consciousness. We are exploring from new perspectives our awareness of the world, ourselves, and the relationship between the two. Our consciousness perceives the world and reflects upon it, imagines the past and the future in the context of the present, and enables us to apprehend ourselves as both within the world and as distinct from it. The interrelationship of human and all other realities in the world creates a uniquely complex and complicated dynamic of human consciousness.

Our vocabulary about ourselves expresses the biases of our history and our contemporary heritage. Our language itself speaks of the intellectual, rational thought, and emotional, affective forces. To identify thinking as emotional or emotions as rational startles us and seems unfamiliar and somehow wrong. Yet if we take seriously the notion that we human beings are a unified whole, then our thought must be affective and our emotions rational.

At this point in the twentieth century, English does not have a clear and easy vocabulary to express the interconnections between thought and feeling. Even the great philosophical explorers of the connection of intellect and feeling in our mental processes still struggle with our feeble vocabulary and inexact analyses.[1] While we await good exploration of the "think-feel" unity of our lives, we also await the vocabulary that will enable us to express what we have discovered.

Shaped by Greek philosophy and empirical science, the dominant culture of the West used to think that it could clearly and rationally explain how we think and express our understanding of ourselves and our world. Human beings have emotions and intellect, the most common interpretation asserted. Our senses perceive the data of the outside world; our intellects enable us to apprehend and interpret this sensory material, and to make judgments about what is true and not true about the external world as well as the way in which the various realities in the world are related.

According to this world view, feelings and the affective and aesthetic dimensions of life are important as a lure to incline us toward the good and to make us more eager to love the truth and avoid evil. The intellect and its rational judgments are, however, of more importance because these judgments determine what we ought to think and do. Therefore the intellect ought to have clear priority over feelings.

In fine-tuning this perspective on human consciousness, we would note that about the time of the Renaissance the dominant educated culture began to identify the empirical scientific and mathematical as the highest form of rational thought, rather than theological and philosophical discourse. During the last few centuries we have retained as fundamental the notion that reality can be best understood through our intellects, with logical judgment as the most important form of knowing. At the center of our twentieth-century European/North

American understanding of human consciousness has firmly stood scientific understanding (sometimes called logical reasoning). Feelings, intuition, artistic expression, and all related ways of expressing something about the world were regarded as clearly inferior to the rational mode of knowing.

In the religious sphere, a challenge to the primacy of intellect in recognizing truth arose in the Great Awakening of the eighteenth century that took so many forms throughout the West: Hassidism, Pietism, Methodism, and the American Great Awakening (mainly in New England). In reaction against the primacy of abstract intellect, various religious figures, such as John Wesley, Count von Zinzendorf, Jonathan Edwards, and the Ba'al Shem Tov, asserted the centrality of another dimension of the person—the affective. But a profound ambivalence toward "enthusiasm" remained even in many of those circles, and frequently abstraction crept back and renewed its reign even in those groups.

In the last few decades Europe and North America have become more aware of the inadequacy of the classical view. They have learned that our perceptions and understandings of the world are formed in far more complicated ways than merely by rational observation and judgment. We have become increasingly receptive to the enormous importance of our more intuitive side, to the centrality of the emotions, and to the way we express our awareness in images, pictures, and stories, which are all laden with feelings as well as intellectual assessments. Our question as preachers is both simple and complex: *How does this shift in awareness of the human spirit and its workings affect the ways we preach the good news of God's activity among us?*

If we wish to be responsible preachers, then we need to appreciate and understand this brave new world we are entering, with its expanding consciousness of our very selves. Otherwise we run the risk of miscommunicating the Gospel instead of proclaiming it, or at least of missing some valuable media for sharing the good news of which we are stewards.

NEW TRENDS IN PREACHING

During the last two decades we have experienced a profound transformation in the way preaching is taught. The use of video equipment is a mere external hint of a profound inner transformation. When one looks at one of the standard older texts, such as John A. Broadus's *On*

the Preparation and Delivery of Sermons, underlying the whole enterprise are the assumptions that human beings are fundamentally
rational creatures, and that the core of the sermon should be a "thesis
statement," normally developed in a syllogism. Certain other variations
on that theme have been suggested and tried, but the primary model
has remained the logical, rational, "three point" sermon.

Recently a different approach has flourished in the mainline of homiletical education. Under the impact of new developments in our understanding of the fundamental importance of the physical and affective,
as well as the intellectual and spiritual in human nature, another style
of preaching is being taught. This approach to preaching focuses on
story, narrative, and the concrete specificity of God's revelation to
human beings in the world. The labors of Eugene Lowrie and Henry
Mitchell are foremost in this change. Their works herald a profound
transformation in preaching, an attempt to take account not only of a
communications theory focusing more on the effectiveness and mem-
orable quality of story, but also a more complex understanding of humanity than older generations of preachers usually worked from.

In order to appreciate the change going on in contemporary preaching, we will be well served by identifying the major developments of
this century that are revolutionizing our ideas about ourselves, our
relationships to others, and the nature of communication.

I have chosen to focus on one specific element of the newer approach
to preaching—imagery and its centrality in preaching. In imagery the
rational and the affective intersect. When we express our consciousness
of the world with images, we incorporate the affective and aesthetic
because imagery represents some concrete and visible thing in the
tangible world. Image embodies a form and appeals to the senses, while
evoking emotions and feelings in us. Imagery also includes an intellectual dimension because the reality the imagery signifies is also in-
vested by us with cognitive meaning. An intellectual analysis of imagery
can relate to many aspects of reality.

Imagery is a more encompassing term than images. Imagery is de-
fined by one editorial team as "the sensory quality of a literary work."[2]
Imagery means more than pictures; it includes the whole physical and
sensory dimension of the world portrayed in a sermon. Frequently one
image will focus all the other imagery or provide the primary sensory
material of the sermon. For instance, in a particular sermon the cross
as the tree of life may be the primary image, with other imagery in

the sermon related to that image (for example, the sermon may mention the time and place where the image was first seen, a tree of death juxtaposed against, and so forth). Imagery includes the whole plastic dimension expressed in the language of a sermon.

Imagery is not the same as story, but the two are intertwined. Story focuses on plot, on the sequence of action and the interconnections among characters and events. Imagery, in the sense I am using the term, presents the physical and visual dimensions of characters, events, and their world. It utters the perspective of "the primary connectedness of human beings to the natural world by fragile and transitory bodies."[3] Narrative and imagery are the two primary foci for human perceptions and interpretations of the world we experience.

One might push the distinction a bit further and suggest that narrative is a primary focus for the more temporally conscious mind, imagery a focus for the spatially and visually directed. But a good narrative demands details and embodiment of imagery, and imagery in preaching is the center and prism for the dramatic narrative that is the very nature of a sermon, which aims both to instruct and to move. Narrative and imagery are two essential complementary parts of the sermonic whole.

My emphasis on imagery comes in part from my conviction that while narrative preaching is the subject of much good work, the use of imagery for the sermon is not so well explored. For instance, a sermon on God *as* rock or God *as* shepherd centers on the depth of imagery, rather than on a story, and on our response to God shaped through that image. Sometimes even a sermon emerging from biblical narrative will center on one dimension of a person and his or her world, a picture or embodied vision. Such a sermon is most helpfully considered from the perspective of imagery.

For us as preachers in the twentieth century, the significance of the image as a representation or an embodiment is very rich. First, our culture is discovering today, from a variety of perspectives, the fundamental importance of concrete, specific imagery in our human perception of and thinking about the world. Television and motion pictures have shaped a visually oriented generation. Abstract, propositional expressions of truth no longer reign supreme in our dominant Western culture. Second, imagery in this sense respects the integrity of the concrete world we are preaching about. We can enjoy all of the specificity and sensory richness of the imagery. At the same time we are also aware of the many rich worlds in which the imagery shares. In the image, the affective and the intellectual are equally focused. Third, as we explore the biblical tradition, we discover that this centrality of imagery and the concrete is not a modern innovation. The Scriptures express themselves primarily in story and imagery. Our new discoveries about the human mind resonate and express in new forms the way the biblical world saw the world and expressed itself.[4]

WHAT IS THE MIND?

During the last hundred years or so, Western consciousness has been transformed by a new awareness of itself. The classical Greek view of the human mind, so influential for centuries in the West, was that humans are rational beings. According to this perspective, we are creatures who possess a powerful reasoning apparatus. This rational capacity is affected by powerful emotions, but intellect properly orders the will and the emotions that are a part of the will. Different theorists have given greater or less substance to the role of the emotions and the will, but all agree that God intended the will and the feelings to be governed by the intellect. People also assumed that we humans are aware of the movements of our will and our intellect. Mind and con-sciousness are essentially the same in this dominant perspective.

Bolstered by such a psychology, the classic sermon form in the West for centuries has been the argument. Whether it is described as "thesis and three points" or "three points and a poem," this style of preaching assumes humans to be rational, fully conscious beings in control of themselves. At the very least, control and full awareness are possible to all people of good will who make the effort.

By the end of the eighteenth century, philosophers (Immanuel Kant for one), and Romantic poets (J. W. Goethe, Samuel Taylor Coleridge, and William Wordsworth) attacked the exaltation of reason in the human person. But Sigmund Freud, the Viennese psychiatrist, convincingly formulated a radical revisioning of the human spirit that overturned the dominant culture's assessment of the human person. Today many parts of Freud's theories are subject to major debate. However, the core of his insight stands fast in contemporary Western psychology. Freud insisted that the realm of conscious, rational reflection, and choice is quite circumscribed. He devised a new explanatory structure of the mind based on notions of id, ego, and superego to express the relatively modest domain of the rational mind in the context of the whole human psyche. His terminology pointed to his conviction that even as we are observing, reflecting, judging, and choosing with conscious awareness, at the same time numerous semiconscious and subconscious energies and patterns from our past operate within us to shape and determine our feelings, responses, and thoughts.

Depth Psychology

Depth psychology insists that the rational human consciousness, which for so many centuries we assumed reigned as supreme in the human person, is merely one force among many in the psyche. Furthermore, rational mind does not dominate, but is shaped if not controlled by various factors to which most of us have little or no access, without complex and lengthy psychoanalysis. Such a vision of humanity, coming so quickly after Charles Darwin's theory of evolution, overthrew the vaunted human claim to biological uniqueness and dethroned human claims to be "rational animals." Human beings didn't reign over themselves, much less over the earth.

Different schools of psychology explain the relationship of conscious to unconscious in different ways. Quite different therapeutic approaches have evolved as Freud's basic insights have encountered different social developments and varying clinical experiences.[5] But contemporary psychology, no matter what direction it takes or what its assessment of various dimensions of Freud's teaching, rests firmly on his rejection of the equation between mind and consciousness, human psyche and rationality.

Depth psychology dwells in that murky realm where we all must admit how little of our mental lives is conscious and rational. Contemporary physics and chemistry also explore with measured precision the interdependence between the brain and our experience of our mind. Over the last few decades, scientists have investigated extensively the physiological basis for emotion, imagination, and rational thought. In light of what remains to be learned, however, science is only at the beginning of its search; it is apparent that brain and mind are not two distinct entities, but clearly related aspects of one whole.

The catch phrase around which much popular awareness of the scientific discussion has centered is "right brain–left brain." Involved in this discussion are some assumptions about the human mind. Experiments have shown that an undoubted connection exists between the body and the mind or spirit, and to some extent that connection can be demonstrated. For instance, in certain experiments a stimulus or shock is administered to a specific part of the brain. Identifiable and predictable reactions occur as a result of the stimulation of the brain. Certain specific skills and abilities do seem connected with certain parts of the brain, with many skills connected with abstract reasoning linked to areas on the left side of the brain, and certain areas related to imagination, affect, and the concrete connected with places on the right side. If specific places in the brain are damaged, predictable skills and abilities are lost.

Various areas of the brain seem to control functions of the body such as walking, moving certain parts of the body, and exchanging certain kinds of physical information. Sometimes one part of the brain can "take over" for another when one section of the brain is damaged. The total process of thought seems to involve functions of both hemispheres of the brain, and when disturbances exist on a biological level, the whole cognitive process is disturbed.

Recently scientists have certainly learned much about the physical aspects of the brain, the connections between the anatomy of the brain and the interaction between chemicals from inside and outside the body, and perceptions of the outside world that the brain receives. These discoveries identify the biological base for the presence of the so-called rational/abstract and the more affective/aesthetic modes of human thought, and some of the ways the two modes work together. As more is discovered, it seems apparent that there are not two kinds of people, rational and logical or intuitive and aesthetic. Even though one aspect may be stronger in one person than in another, each person possesses capacities for human thought. These capacities as a whole incorporate dimensions of both aspects of cognition. Both intuitive and affective are essential to complete human thought, and a biological base exists for asserting that the human mind uses and requires these dimensions.[6]

Thought Processes and Decision Making

We have also recently witnessed a growth in exploring the ways in which people learn and make decisions, as in the field of moral development. The twentieth century has seen remarkable changes in developmental psychology. Students of human behavior, such as Jean Piaget, have explored how people grow and change in their ways of perceiving the world and ordering their experiences. Recent years have seen a growing interest not only in intellectual development, but also in moral growth.

Lawrence Kohlberg has outlined a complex system to identify how human beings grow from creatures exclusively concerned with themselves and their own comfort into persons aware of others and their rights and needs, persons who are finally capable of making moral judgments on the basis of abstract principles of good and evil. For Kohlberg, who is widely regarded as one of the greatest researchers in this field, the ability to make moral decisions on the basis of abstract principles is the highest stage of moral development. One of Kohlberg's former students, Carol Gilligan, noted that the subjects whose test results formed the basis for Kohlberg's norms were all male. She tested females as well as males and noted that the results did tend toward a specific difference. Whereas males usually moved to a stage of making judgments on the basis of abstract principles, females continued to base their decisions on increasingly complex assessments of interpersonal situations and the impact of decisions on the persons involved. Gilligan suggests that rather than judging one approach to be inferior or superior to the other, we are best served by acknowledging the differences and refusing to assert, as Kohlberg does, that the abstract is always to be preferred to the concrete human interrelationship. In certain situations the specific is more helpful, and even the abstract principle is shaped and changed by a sensitive appraisal of the individual situation.[7]

Even in the realm of philosophy of science, theorists have become increasingly aware of the limits of human rationality. From writing and discussion about models and modes of scientific thought emerges an awareness that at its heart the scientific enterprise does not depend exclusively on deductive, logical, rational movement from one clearly discerned step to another. The origin of original scientific thought seems to emerge from an intuitive jump, the insight which grasps a vision of the whole rather than being concerned primarily with quantitative measures and judgments.

Increasingly, scientists are aware that the scientific world view perceives reality in pictures and patterns. Images and models of the universe show our imaginations what all or a dimension or part of reality is like. On the basis of that vision, we can begin to formulate the rational, precise experiments and hypotheses that give body and empirical content to the scientific vision. Contemporary scientists and philosophers seem more aware than ever before of the unarticulated but real intuitive/affective aspects of the scientific enterprise.[8]

INSIGHTS FROM OTHER CULTURES

In the twentieth century we have become self-consciously aware that our way of explaining and interpreting the human mind is partial. Other people see it differently. Cultural relativity is now a part of twentieth-century awareness. We know and to some degree value the fact that other human beings on earth neither perceive the world nor express themselves about it in the same way that we do. These differences do not consist merely in verbal translation, but are rooted in perceptions and evaluations of the world that are fundamentally distinct from those of the rational, empirical approach that has so long dominated in the West.

Contemporary communications and transportation alert us to the value of these different visions of the cosmos, both in other parts of the globe and at home, among native peoples whom we have generally ignored or devalued. Many people have written and spoken about these relative world views. One of the most incisive is Jamake Highwater, of Blackfoot/Cherokee heritage. In *The Primal Mind* he attempts to recount the perspective of native peoples, who experience and describe the world differently from those who belong exclusively to the dominant culture.[9]

Highwater's chief assertion is both simple and complex. Human beings have two basic ways of envisaging the world, he suggests. One can see these embodied in cultures, but also in perspectives on the world present in every culture. For the West in general, the two approaches are focused in science and art. Science articulates for us a mode of thinking that explores the universe in experiment and in equation, assuming that the truly real can be quantified and measured, and is best expressed in rational, logical, and abstract formulations. Art aspires to intuit the world in its totality and to express some dimension of the interrelated whole. In tactile, concrete forms it embodies a universal insight. In science reason is primary; in art affect is.

For many Westerners, rooted in centuries-old preferences, science is the primary, and certainly the most valued form of thinking. It is better because it offers us clear and certain truths about the world we agree is really there. Art is too "soft"; it can give us only a private vision. It tells us about what we feel or what might be there. Even if art is enriching to an individual, it makes no impact on the way we structure our lives as a community or as a culture.

True as this approach may be for many in the West, for others it is not necessarily self-evident. In many cultures, especially the ones Highwater calls primal, (such as the native cultures in the U.S. and other nations), art is the primary mode of perception. The aesthetic mode provides a vision of reality as a whole. The totality is always primary. That which is quantified and measured is always secondary. When the primal mind looks at image, time, place, motion, or sound, it seeks to appreciate the interrelationships in the cosmic whole.

Such a vision opens itself to the sacred, the holy that is present in and interpenetrates the ordinary, perceptible world but cannot be quantified or measured. Highwater speaks of the capacity to "see twice" to which an elder encouraged him. First, said the elder, you must look about you and see everything together, and see each thing clearly. Then, said the elder, you must "look at the edge of what is visible." You must learn to see dimly so as to perceive the visions and the cloud people who are also there.[10] The primal sees the whole—visible and invisible, the world and the sacred—all of which are here together, even if not in a scientifically verifiable mode.

The primal mind seeks to perceive the whole, and to identify the relationships among things as primary. Time for the primal mind, for example, is not fundamentally the measurement of the duration of physical change. Time is the realm in which human beings exist. Rather than using history as a primary category and focusing on present, past, or future, objective measures of change are not relevant notions. For instance, at the same time one is in a specific place on earth, one can also contact the realm of the ancestors or even of the gods. Mythological language speaks of "piercing the sky," and the primal mind imagines no contradiction in being in two worlds at one and the same "time."[11]

A specific object, such as a rock, a piece of grass, or a snake, is not only a perceptible, measurable item at this specific time in this place. Because the whole universe is interconnected, a rock is not only itself, but also in some sense is all rocks; it is also an expression of the sacred power and stability upholding the universe. But if the rock is in a particular shape—for instance, like the back and neck of a deer—it may also manifest the swiftness and grace of the deer, and be of great importance in hunting magic. Many different dimensions of reality can be united in this one image because of the interconnectedness of all reality.

Are these two visions of the world mutually exclusive? Are they evolutionary stages in humanity's search for truth? Highwater proposes a quite different assessment. Increasingly, we have reached a wide-spread acknowledgement of the inadequacy of the scientific world view. Various peoples whose perspective would be called "primal" have long recognized that for some dimensions of knowing reality, the post-Enlightenment scientific perspective is invaluable. To some extent each person already looks at the world with both perspectives, and gains a fuller perspective on reality by doing so.

The artist and scientist live side by side in our world. One knows how to measure and quantify and believe that which can be empirically proven, and the other seeks a vision of the whole in which sacred and profane, animal and human, intellect and heart are all one interconnected unity. If we are to be fully human, then we must learn how to see the world both ways, aesthetically and scientifically, Highwater suggests, with our primal mind and our rational scientific mind. On this path lies the way to personal and global survival.

In raising his cry, Highwater picks up themes that resonate with contemporary scientists and theorists, who are intensely aware that all creativity and insight involve elements of the primal mind as well as the rational scientific approach. From a multicultural approach, he identifies the same need for reappropriation and appreciation for the value of thought not dominated by abstraction and scientific criteria for truth, but open to other intuitive/affective approaches.

CONTEMPORARY
THEOLOGICAL DEVELOPMENTS

Several strands of theology today challenge the dominance of rationality in Western thought. At least since the twelfth century when theology started to make its home in the universities of France and Italy, systematic (scientific, in the classical sense) theology claimed to be the only acceptable form of theology for thoughtful Christians. However, systematic theology no longer reigns unchallenged in the theological world. Much less is it "the Queen of the Sciences." Two particular strands of contemporary theology suggest that the scientific rational mode is not the only way to be theological. One is liberation theology, which takes various forms in Latin America, Asia, and Africa.

The other is feminist theology, a specific type of liberation theology. Feminist and liberation theologians insist that experience is the beginning point of theology, and that passion and involvement as part of the theological enterprise are not evils to be eschewed, but intrinsic goods to be sought and incorporated into the theological process.[12]

Latin American liberation theology arose from an experience of the domination of peasant and working classes by a ruling elite using physical violence, social oppression, and deprivation of all means of participation in the political and social process to subordinate the lower classes. Out of the masses' experience of exclusion and tyranny has grown a theology that focuses on God's action in the world. God works, these theologians claim, to free people. God's freedom is not metaphorical, abstract, or otherworldly. God wills to free people from those specific evils that oppress, bind, twist, or destroy them in the present. Liberation theology concerns itself with delivering people from all that prevents them from living a fully human life.

The crucified and risen Jesus is *the central image* of liberation theology. This figure expresses in itself the suffering and oppression even to death experienced by the people, and also the confidence that resurrection, change, and transformation can occur through God's activity. In Jesus, infinite pain and unbounded expectation for God's future in the world are united as one reality, embodying the ultimate interconnection of divine and human life.

Feminist theology, which is strongest in North America and Europe, can nonetheless be found around the globe. It roots itself specifically in the experiences of women. Because in all cultures women of various classes are treated as inferior to men, all women share an experience of oppression—even though its particular shape and context may differ. Perhaps the universal, almost ontological, dimension of women's oppression encourages feminist theology to articulate its particularly characteristic contribution to theology as a whole.[13]

But at the same time women are conscious of their oppression, they are psychically and biologically aware of their interconnectedness with the process of life. Their experience centers them in an awareness of being an interconnected part of the whole of creation. Creation forms a totality with God. Even though it may be fractured and twisted in its relationships, it still forms a whole. As human beings discern and develop the interrelationships between God and each other, they find the fullness of reality.

Feminist theology suggests ways human beings can overcome hostilities and divisions based on class and race. Frequently liberation theology identified class and race divisions as setting people at enmity with one another. Feminist theology usually sees enmity and oppression in the context of an interlocking network of oppression. It asserts that each of us is involved in interconnected webs of oppression in which we play different parts. For instance, the same male peasant farmer who is unjustly beaten by government soldiers may in turn go home and beat his wife to keep her in subjection to him. Feminist theology asserts unequivocally that God's freedom offered to this creation involves our seeing and affirming that which unites us as children of God seeking freedom. But liberation also necessitates recognizing and breaking those chains connecting us as participants in oppression of ourselves and others. Freedom emerges in the liberation of all people, with respectful and nurturing living in the world, that the world of creation may become a living unity in God.

In its ideal of freedom, liberation theology also includes an ecological dimension. Human liberation and the development of humanity are fundamental, but because we are all a part of the whole of creation, we also must take account of nature. The scientific view, which objectifies nature, can serve to bolster the dominance and exploitation of nature, which it regards as a nonhuman thing, to be used for whatever purpose powerful human beings choose. Feminist theology rejects such a destructive attitude toward nature, asserting that we are part of an organic unity with the rest of nature. Nature is to be respected and cared for, not used and discarded solely for our benefit, as though our being were totally separate from its. All of creation is an interrelated whole with God—human, animal, vegetable, and mineral. The feminist theological perspective is global in the fullest sense.

Feminist theology energetically rejects (methodologically) the dominance of abstraction, rational discourse, and quantifiable thinking to the exclusion of the affective, the intuitive, the aesthetic appreciation of the world. On the contrary, many feminist theologians insist that intuitive thought is more adequate and more fundamental to theology than abstract, rational discourse. Common to all feminist theologians is the insistence on human wholeness in knowing. Feminists insist that cognitive and affective, physical and mental, participate in one process through which we perceive, understand, and love the world.

IMPACT ON PREACHING

It should now be clear that we are living, working, and preaching in a world in which we express and explain ourselves in more complex ways than ever before. Furthermore, today we understand and describe our own consciousness in more nuanced and richer ways than have ever before been possible. For preachers, moreover, such a recognition requires us to acknowledge that the preaching of the past, which focused on the intellectual, the academic, and the rational, is still valuable and contributes to an essential dimension of the homiletic endeavor. Such an approach, however, is incomplete.

Today's preachers must take account of developments in human self-awareness and communication, or else they handicap their efforts to communicate the good news. The concern during the last few years about preaching in the narrative mode (story) and imagery evidences preachers' efforts to explore the interconnection between new insights into humanity and our proclamation of the gospel.

My intention in the remainder of this book is to focus on specific ways in which images are central to the Bible's vision of God. How can images function this way in our own preaching today? How can we best shape our sermons to weave images into the fabric of our preaching?

2
Biblical Imagery

We of the twentieth century are not the first to recognize how important images are as meaning bearers. We are merely more self-aware of the significance of imagery. Over the centuries, imagery has been a vital element in preaching, teaching, and theology. For the Christian preacher, the Bible provides the center of the understanding and use of imagery. If we are able to grasp confidently the varied ways in which the Scriptures use imagery, we will have rediscovered, reclaimed, and reintegrated into our lives a buried tradition that will enrich our perception and proclamation of the gospel.

THE BIBLICAL WORLD VIEW

The books of the Bible were produced during a period of over a thousand years. To speak in a simple way about "the biblical world view" is a foolish and futile enterprise. Over the course of its biblical history, Israel changed from a semi-nomadic to an agricultural society with a growing population. Over centuries, Egyptian, Canaanite, Philistine, Assyrian, Babylonian, Persian, Hellenistic, and Roman cultures shaped and influenced the Jewish vision of the world and of God.

Furthermore, the writings in the Bible include history, hymns, wisdom literature, prophetic oracles, poetry, letters, and so forth. Thus the Scriptures encompass greatly varied modes of expression, use diverse sorts of images, draw from various historical contexts with various intentions, and span a great chronological spectrum of thousands of years. To describe "the biblical world view" would seem to be an illusory effort.

Even though all these cautions are true, some fundamental dimensions of the world view of the ancient Israelites endured over the centuries. For our purposes the most important elements of the Hebrew world view are not the specifics of cosmology, knowledge of flora and fauna, political perspectives, and so forth.[1] Underlying the complexities of the Hebrew vision of the world are certain fundamental perceptions about the constitution of the visible world and its relationship to God. Three themes emerge as particularly important for appreciating how Israelites used imagery.

1. Everything is alive, part of one living creation, obedient to God. We moderns have something of a counterpart in the contemporary physics that insists that the same energy present on the atomic level in a rock or in the soil also is in a person. Various forms in the world are different permutations and complex organizations of the same fundamental energy.

In an exploration of the meaning of contemporary physics for us, Nick Herbert observes:

> Religions assure us that we are all brothers and sisters, children of the same deity; biologists say that we are entwined with all the life-forms on this planet: our fortunes rise or fall with theirs. Now, physicists have discovered that the very atoms of our bodies are woven out of a common super-luminal fabric. Not merely in physics are humans out of touch with reality; we ignore these connections at our peril.[2]

In Genesis 1 we hear the ancient religious version of this vision of the living unity of all creation. God creates the heavens and the earth, and all the things which dwell therein. Because it is God's creation, everything that exists can respond to and praise God. "God is king! Let the earth rejoice! . . . The heavens proclaim God's saving justice, all nations see God's glory" (Ps. 97:1, 6). "Praise God, sun and moon; praise God, all shining stars; praise God, highest heavens; praise God, waters above the heavens. . . . Praise Yahweh from the earth . . . mountains and every hill, orchards and every cedar, wild animals and all cattle, reptiles and winged birds, old people and children together" (Ps. 148:3, 7, 9, 10, 12). Many books of the Hebrew Bible are filled with rich imagery of creation's activity praising its creative God. Who else, asks God of Job, laid the earth's cornerstone "to the joyful concert of the morning stars"(Job 38:7).

The biblical perspective excludes numerous minor deities under a supreme deity, or a heaven of coequal divinities. Yahweh is the sole God of Israel. But this alternate perspective is not of a one-dimensional cosmos of inert matter, but a living community of trees and rocks and animals and humans and angels, each sharing in some way life from

God and the capacity to return praise to the divine creator. Personification and imagery thus are not mere poetic window dressing, but reflect a profound religious and theological conviction about the nature of the world.

2. The Hebrews perceived a continuity of meaning from a concrete image to a more abstract interpretation. That is, one might say that the ancient Israelites did not usually make such abstract statements as: In the last days, when God restores us from exile back to our homeland, we will become very prosperous. Rather, the prophet or poet would sing: "The plowman will tread on the heels of the reaper, and the threader of grapes on the heels of the sower of seed, and the mountains will run with new wine and all the hills flow with it" (Amos 9:13).

One might call Amos's language poetic and (from a contemporary perspective) be correct. Poetry expresses universal truths in a concrete form, so that in good poetry one does indeed see "the universe in a grain of sand." But for the ancient Hebrew, our distinction between prose and poetry did not exist, and our categories are somewhat anachronistic. All writing was to some extent poetic, for it expressed the story of the people's experience of God in concrete, specific story or image. The language of narrative (prose), the direct expression of experience is found on every page of Scripture.

Sometimes this specific language serves primarily to accentuate the force of statements (e.g., "For evil doers will be annihilated, while those who hope in Yahweh shall have the land for their own," Ps. 37:10). The capacity of the concrete image to evoke the cosmic truth always stems from our acknowledgment that each part of the universe is a piece of the whole, with every part interrelated. A part of the world can represent the whole; specific characteristics or images stand for a whole state of being.

For instance, one does not say, "Good people will be rewarded by God." Instead, one prays that "those who hope in Yahweh," those who are in a trusting relationship with God, will "possess the land for their own." That is, they will live in and prosper through a relationship to that very land God promised to the ancestors. Everything in the image is very concrete and specific, even though its meaning is clearly a universal statement about the absoluteness of God's faithfulness and the sure reward promised to those who keep the covenant with God.

Every concrete image or event is "open" in the sense that it is itself and what it appears to be, but it is also more. Because it is part of an interconnected world, the image-event contains potentially in itself the capacity to represent universal reality and sometimes even the universe itself.

3. We Westerners have assimilated fairly well the logical dictum of noncontradiction: No reality can be judged true and false at the same time with respect to the same quality. Although we cannot wisely read Greek logic back into Hebrew literature, we quickly discover the Bible's elasticity in its willingness to include several different explanations of the same reality. These different explanations are accepted even if on the surface (or perhaps more deeply) they appear contradictory.

We find an obvious example in the accounts of creation. In Genesis, we find that the editors have placed back-to-back two distinct accounts of the same event (Gen. 1:1—2:3 and 2:4b-25). No matter what critical explanation we moderns accept, we are confronted with the phenomenon of a priestly editor who was not at all troubled by putting a hieratic, poetic account of ordered creation (by a God whose mere word causes everything to emerge according to the divine will) side-by-side with a vivid anthropomorphic story. In the second account in Gen. 2:4b-25 (Yahwist), the focus is on humanity; God has to act physically to create; and God experiments before finding the right partner for Adam. No matter how one explains these differences, they are profound, and offer quite different views on God's way of creating relationship with creation and on the very nature of the creation itself.

But the final editor of Genesis accepted and the Hebrew people preserved and revered as "true" both images of God's creative relationship with the world. No one seemed concerned with any sense of contradiction of these two versions of the same event as true expressions of God's revelation. Rather than accusing the ancient biblical works and readers of intellectual deficiency or inferiority, we recognize that their world view accepted the possibility of different, even apparently incongruent, aspects of reality as all being true at the same time.

In this biblical perspective, reality is not a one-dimensional phenomenon to be observed according to immutable laws, but a multi-faceted story that can be entered into, told, and heard from varying perspectives. It is a world far closer to Jamake Highwater's "multiverse," in which realities assume different relationships and forms depending on the perspective in which they are viewed, rather than the "universe" of mathematical logic.

OLD TESTAMENT IMAGES

The world view of the Bible is much closer to the "primal" mind of Highwater's description than to the "scientific" vision he contrasts with it. Biblical communication roots itself deeply in a world in which intellect and affect, thought and feeling, are closely linked, in which all of reality is alive and interconnected, and in which we share as a part of this multidimensional whole.

A preacher who wants to preach to the whole person will find such a world congenial because its language is imaginative, grasping people at the place in their hearts and minds where the intellect and the emotions meet, where we at once think and feel and act. But the preacher needs to be prepared to engage in a complex encounter, because the dynamic that imagery sets up is a different form of discourse from the more familiar form of the logician or scientist.

As preachers or teachers explore various images used in the Scriptures for God (and the corresponding images used or implied for human beings), they notice at once the common, ordinary character of these images. At once the hearer is thrust into a strange new territory in which the atmosphere is, as the ancient Celts called it, "thin." That is, everything observable is familiar, day-to-day common stock, what we all know and use. At the same time, this reality is bearer and sign of another divine reality, which at any moment may break through and speak to the hearer. The divine and the ordinary constantly interplay with each other. The hearer is invited to be open to a world in which God may be present *through* such basic realities as a lamp or a rock or a shepherd's crook. God is present in and through the commonplace, and the ordinary discloses God.

At the same time the communicator is aware of the presence of God in the ordinary, the preacher also notes that such images are used in an iconoclastic way. God is present in a rock, but God is not a rock, nor is God adequately present only as a rock. God is present but not contained in or adequately represented by the image. Any given image is in itself incomplete, a true representative only up to a point. It both bears the divine presence and at the same time breaks open under the richness of divine life. In this sense the image is both icon and iconoclastic, representing the divine and unable to represent it.

Such limitation presses the preacher to acknowledge that each image in itself is incomplete. To make any one image absolute or even to fix upon one as primary is to strain to the breaking point the power of imagery. Only through a variety of images does the Hebrew Scripture present God's interaction with human beings. Only through the exploration and use of many different images is the divine reality presented to the people. The preacher is invited by the Scriptures to follow the same example. As we will see, each sermon does not need to include every possibly related image. But as we create the sermon and preach it, our voice, words, and gestures will proclaim the limits as well as the possibilities of the imagery we present.

As we explore the Scriptures for imagery used about God, we find rich resources that enable us to identify various images and their role in Scripture. These resources include concordances, dictionaries, specialized studies of imagery, and themes in the Scriptures.[3] None of these works can expose the preacher to the richness of the imagery, but they can alert one to the locations of specific images, contexts, and parallels in other parts of Scripture and in ancient Middle Eastern culture. Once these images are located, the preacher enters into the dynamic dialogue of learning about and seeing the image, reflecting on it, and relating it to other parts of the Scripture and to contemporary life.

Even a cursory glance at the range of images used for God in the Old Testament shows a significant array of persons and things used to express aspects of God's self-revelation. The preacher who considers even a few will become aware of rich possibilities.

Rock. One of the most vivid biblical images for God is that of a rock. The stability, power, and apparent constant eternity of the great rocks and mountains of the land suggested to the biblical people a God who also was stable, powerful, eternal, and a place of refuge. "He is the rock, his work is perfect, for all his ways are equitable" (Deut. 32:4).

The Psalms are particularly full of rock and mountain images for God. As Othmar Keel notes, in this image of rock the Psalms combine the image of God as the rock of power and refuge with the figure of the Temple rock.[4] Psalm 18 focuses on the Rock of refuge and strength: "Yahweh is my rock and fortress. . . . I take refuge in him, my rock. . . . You lift me high above those who attack me, you deliver me from the man of violence." Psalm 28 links rock and temple (the temple built on the rock of Mt. Zion) directly in parallel verses: "To you, Yahweh, I cry, my rock, do not be deaf to me! . . . Hear the sound of my prayer when I call upon you, when I raise my hands, Yahweh, towards your Holy of Holies" (vv. 1-2).

Light. In the figure of God as light, a quite different emphasis emerges. God as light is important both for the cosmos and for the individual. God as light transforms the natural function of one of the natural forces into the divine pledge of a new creation, in which God is the center of all. "No more will the sun give you daylight, nor moonlight shine on you, but Yahweh will be your everlasting light, and God will be your everlasting splendor" (Isa. 60:19). God as light both replaces the old natural forces and is a pledge of a new and glorious existence that is no longer subject to the inadequacies of time.

The Psalms especially contain abundant imagery of God as light: "Yahweh is my light and my salvation, whom should I fear?" (Ps. 27:1). "In you is the source of life, by your light we see the light" (Ps. 36:9). God is not only a provider of cosmic change but also the one who guides and gives wisdom and aid to the individual. Light not only protects, but it also enables and empowers God's faithful to act.

Parent. In the Old Testament itself there is remarkably little parent imagery about God, particularly if one contrasts it with imagery related to other human figures such as the king. The use of the term "father" is direct, when it occurs; "mother" imagery is usually more indirect. Father imagery usually is connected with protection and acceptance, especially the forgiveness of sins; mother imagery is linked with nurturance and care.

In Psalm 103, for example, "As tenderly as a father treats his children, so Yahweh treats those who fear him; he knows of what we are made, he remembers that we are dust" (vv. 13-14). In Isaiah 64 we find, "For you have hidden your face from us and given us up to the power of our misdeeds. And yet, Yahweh, you are our father" (vv. 6-7).

Mother imagery is linked in part with the formula for God, "Yahweh the merciful and gracious," in which the word for merciful is derived from the word for womb—the abstract plural *rhmym* from *rhmh*.[5] Yahweh's mercy is motherlove, the compassion of a mother for the child she has borne. In Jeremiah 31, in the midst of the passage (vv. 15-23), Yahweh contrasts Rachel's mourning for her dead children with Yahweh's own remembrance of Ephraim, the "dear son" (v. 20) who will be found and restored. At other times Yahweh is compared to the mother laboring to bring forth Israel: "I have kept quiet, held myself in check, groaning like a woman in labor, panting and gasping for air" (Isa. 42:14).

Maker. God the maker or creator shows God as the all-powerful source and governor of all that is. Instead of focusing on God's immediate concern for the involvement with each and every one, the creator image stresses the cosmic and corporate dimension of God's relationship to the world. Genesis 1 and 2 portray God as the maker of the world who speaks, or in the second account, who molds the clay, and everything comes to be according to the divine plan.

Elihu assures Job that "God's was the spirit that made me, and Shaddai's the breath that gave me life" (Job 33:4). God's whole "answer" to Job's questioning is an extended metaphor of the wisdom of God the maker (Job 38–40). One of the many prophetic references to God's creative activity occurs in the story of Jeremiah's visit to the potter, in which the prophet sees in the potter's working a reflection of God's creative activity, forming and reforming us (Jer. 18:1-12). Psalm 104 and Genesis 1–2 express God's universal creativity in great detail, as the divine bounty produces the heavens and the earth and all living creatures, as well as the seasons and the movements of all that lives on earth.

Judge. God's creativity is not simply the bounty of a fertility deity. God is a just God, who creates the world in and for the righteous. One of the most frequent images for God is that of judge. In Genesis 18, for instance, when Yahweh plans to destroy Sodom and Gomorrah, Abraham pleads with him as "the judge of the whole world" (v. 25). Jephthah appeals to "Yahweh the Judge" in his conflict with the Ammonites (Judg. 11:27).

In Psalm 82 we see a vivid portrait of God the sovereign judge standing in the midst of the divine assembly. In biblical thought, God's role as the divine judge is connected with the divine sovereignty. God sees the injustice and oppression of the poor and the weak in the world, and is begged to rectify the world's injustice: "Arise, God, judge the world, for all nations belong to you" (v. 8). Psalm 94 echoes the same expectation: "Arise, judge of the world, give back the proud what they deserve" (v. 2).

Warrior.   Even though many of us today are quite uncomfortable with the notion of a warrior God, for the ancient Hebrews this image was an essential component of the idea of God as creator and judge. A God without the power to enforce judgment and make righteousness was unimaginable. Whether the warrior God is the one who leads the people into the land and strengthens them to drive out the Canaanites, or the one who would strike down the enemies of good and righteousness all over the earth, the warrior carried out the divine decrees and made effective God's wisdom and compassionate justice.

Miriam and all the Israelites acclaim the warrior who frees the slaves: "Sing to Yahweh, for he has covered himself in glory, horse and rider he has thrown into the sea" (Exod. 15:20-21). Psalm 24 connects the king and the warrior motif: "Who is he, the king of glory? It is Yahweh, strong and valiant, Yahweh, valiant in battle" (v. 10). Psalm 78 presents God as the covenant sovereign of Israel who can spare the people and also lead them to victory, but can also deliver them to destruction and "vent his wrath on the people" (v. 59). But the primary focus of the warrior image remains God as liberator: "For the Lord is a God who breaks battle lines; he has pitched his camp in the middle of his people to deliver me from the hands of my oppressors" (Jth. 16:2).

EXPLORING THE IMAGERY

Each of these images as well as others (e.g., God as way, shepherd, friend) has its own rich content and context. In the process of drawing upon the biblical image in a sermon, the preacher will want to proceed from literary analysis of the written words about the imagery to hearing the imagery speak to contemporary life. One needs to read, hear, and see the textual performance, although any one of us may find one approach of special help at different times or with various texts.

Imagery with its depth and multivalence, its revelatory character, is not directly transparent to us. We do not always know the world of the Bible, we do not always listen or look carefully, we sometimes do not make direct or honest connections between biblical realities and our world. Because the Scripture is not self-evident to us, we need an interpretive device to discover the appropriate connections to see, and how best to enter empathetically into the biblical world.[6]

In the process of hearing and responding to the images, many questions will occur to the preacher to enable her or him to understand better the various images and the sensory dimension of the Scriptures, to perceive its significance for the church today, and to imagine various ways to express today God's self-revelation given to the biblical imagery. As a result of our encounter with biblical imagery, five questions seem to me to be of special importance in discerning contemporary helpfulness of images:

1. *What is the root of this image in common human experience?* If God is my light, what does it mean to have light? As I walk down a dark alleyway and suddenly am flooded by the clarity and safety of a strong street lamp, I not only am able to see, but feel sure of my way and my safety. A sunrise is also light, but with different meaning and evoking somewhat different feelings. A flashlight is also a light; it guides and offers awareness to us in situations in which we would otherwise be helpless. Unless our eyes are totally unable to perceive light, we all have some experience of being enabled to be aware of and in contact with the world in a new way. Light evokes our ability to see, and gives us knowledge, safety, and a connection with the world about us and with our own bodies.

2. *How does this image portray God?* If our central image of God is as judge, our primary perception of God is as the one who made the world to exist in justice, with all creatures in right relationships to one another and to God. God is concerned with power in relationships, with assuring that the just are not oppressed, that the poor and helpless are not shortchanged or cheated. As in all ancient Near Eastern government, separation of powers does not prevail; God as judge is the one who intends justice, makes judgments, and enforces them.

3. *What does this image imply about God's relationship to human beings?* Our images of God shape the way in which we perceive and respond to God. In relationship to a judge, we are clients and defendants, who have wrongs to be redressed, and who have sometimes done wrong that deserves to be punished. On a broader scale, we are participants in the judge's effort to bring about a righteous world, and we rejoice as justice is done (Luke 18:1-8). If God as parent is our central focus, we are primarily dependents and children, though we certainly can see ourselves as adult children. In the ancient Hebrew world, even independent adults were still children of their parents, bound by legal and moral bonds, and in return expecting certain care as well as offering reverence and service.

4. *What response to God does this image evoke in the hearer?* Evocations are subjective, but certain images certainly tend to elicit

specific responses from us. For example, to pray to God as my rock invites me to imagine security, stability, and protection. If God is my rock, I feel safer, as though I am protected from my enemies and secure to do what I need to (as in Martin Luther's "A Mighty Fortress"). But to tell me that God is my sovereign, my king, asks me to jump to attention, to reconsider my loyalties, and to look to God as being in charge of my life. God could ask me to do or not do something, and has claims on me, as well as owing me protection and guidance.

5. *How is this image complemented by other images?* Few images for God stand alone. For instance in Psalm 103, God is the one who forgives offenses, "as tenderly as a father treats his children" (v. 13), but is also the sovereign who has "fixed his throne in heaven, and whose "sovereign power rules over all" (v. 19). God as parent and God as sovereign complement each other. God is not only a sovereign who is charged with the welfare and right behavior, but also rules from heaven, with a comprehensive view of the whole. God is also like a compassionate parent who is intimately involved with each person, who expects the best of each one, but remembers our weakness and limitations, and forgives. To see God only as sovereign might inspire dread and awe, but no attraction or love. To portray God only as parent might encourage love and devotion, but might also become sentimental or individualized. When the two images are placed together, God is seen to be both powerful and tender, attentive to all and careful of each, loving and awesome.

Use of complementary images can be particularly helpful in clarifying and carefully shaping particularly powerful images. No image is universally experienced by everyone unambiguously. Sometimes the sun's head is not just refreshing and invigorating (life-giving); it can also overcome and kill the weak or susceptible (life-ending). Some people have loving fathers, others dreadful ones; some individuals experience a judge as the embodiment of the injustice of an oppressive government, others know the judge as one who applies good laws equitably.

We can try to say what we mean by an image (e.g., the sun is primarily beneficent in our experience). But we convey our meaning more completely and powerfully if we can put two or more images together (e.g., God is the sun of righteousness, whose just judgments bring peace and prosperity to the earth). Complementary images can shape and give specificity to each other. For instance, God is sun and judge. The sun's abundance modified by the judge imagery suggests that we focus on the constructive and ordering capacities of the sun as live-giver. By putting judge in the context of sun, the all-encompassing quality of God's justice is expressed.

The Old Testament portrays a God as we see a diamond—complex, many faceted, a prism reflecting and refracting different colors and images from the world around us. From an apparently infinite number of angles the diamond displays a different aspect of its richness to us. Yahweh is known through many images, evoking quite distinct, sometimes complementary and sometimes apparently contradictory responses (e.g., God as parent and as warrior). Yet for the Hebrews, each is necessary and none alone is adequate.

THE NEW TESTAMENT

The New Testament offers another dimension to the envisioning of God. In Genesis we hear that humans are created in the image of God (*imago Dei*). We are thus assured that humanity, as God intended it to be, reflects something of what God is. Some of the later rabbis suggested that humanity's being in God's image consists of exercising kingly guidance over creation, as God does over us. The Christian tradition has assumed that intellectual and decision-making powers reflect the divine being, and that they are the "divine image" in us. This interpretation has been rooted in a fundamental certainty that God could be imaged here and now, and that humanity provided a focus for this imaging.

In the New Testament, the figure of Jesus adds a new dimension to the idea of humanity in God's image. In light of our fallenness and inadequacy, Jesus is regarded as the unique and normative image of God who has come to restore us (John 1:14, 18; Luke 10:22; 2 Cor. 4:4-6; Col. 1:15-16; Heb. 1:3). For the preacher, the significance of this explanation of image is that the restored humanity embodied in Jesus is proclaimed a true image of God's love and God's glory. We are intended to be re-created in the image of Christ—in effect, to be the image of the Image (e.g., Rom. 8:29; 2 Cor. 3:18; 1 John 3:2). Thus our human being is affirmed as the locus for a real and true—even if finite and not-yet-perfected—reflection of God's reality.

This biblical theological framework is central to developments in the Christian tradition that focus on both human sharing in the divine life through imaging God made known to us in Christ, and in seeing in all of creation what Saint Augustine called *vestigia Dei*, the "footsteps" of

God. Augustine declared that all creation in some sense mirrored God, because all creation shared in our relationship to God.

Recovery of aspects of these traditions is invaluable for the contemporary preacher.[7] Exploration of the New Testament pushes us to acknowledge the interconnection between divine and human that can best be expressed in a more complete theology of image. At the same time the Bible insists on distinction between God and creation, it also insists on their essential interconnection.

JESUS' USE OF IMAGERY

Jesus was a Jew, and the New Testament expresses a largely Jewish world view, as well as reflecting some of the encounter between Jewish perspectives and Gentile questioning and reinterpretation. Furthermore, in the New Testament the Scriptures are the Old Testament—the Hebrew Bible. Consequently, it is no surprise that the basic imagery of the New Testament, as well as the way this imagery is used, is fundamentally Jewish, and in continuity with the Old Testament.

But because so much of our preaching is focused through the Gospels, and specifically in Jesus, certain aspects of his use of imagery in the New Testament are central for us. Perhaps most significant is the acknowledgment that Jesus' imagery about God and about himself is derived from the Hebrew Scriptures, either directly or indirectly. Jesus' teaching is, like that of the Hebrew Bible, full of and dependent on imagery, not linear or scientific logic. Jesus does not teach organized systematic theology; he proclaims the good news through concrete and specific images.

Jesus expresses his own understanding of himself through images from the Old Testament. In Matt. 23:37-39, for example, he uses the protective parent and God as eagle imagery to express his relationship with Jerusalem. In John 8 he calls himself the light of the world, linking together the images of God as light and the Law as light or lamp (e.g., Ps. 119:105), and implying his own connection with God and the law. Some of the images Jesus uses about himself link him specifically with the messianic tradition. Examples include the lamb (John 1:29, 19:36-37), with its Passover significance (Exod. 12:1-14; Jer. 11:19; Isa. 53:7-12), or the temple (2 Kings 7; Matt. 21:12-17; John 7:37-39).

In using this imagery, Jesus (for his interpreters) clearly links himself and his own awareness of himself and his mission with the Hebrew Bible. All Christians must interpret Jesus in this context if they wish to understand his person and message rightly, but a faithful preacher must take care to hear and see Jesus in this Jewish world.

For instance, when preaching about the good shepherd, one must ask first how Jesus probably intended this image to be received. What was a shepherd in first century Palestinian society? What Old Testament references to shepherds might Jesus have had in mind—all the references to God as the Shepherd of Israel, kings and priests as shepherds, and the many other references? How do these references (the historic weight of the image) shape Jesus' perception of himself and his mission? Why does he use this image in a particular context? To short-circuit a thorough exploration of biblical imagery in its own integrity is to risk misinterpreting it.

In being attentive to Jesus' own use of imagery or to imagery attributed to him, one should also be sensitive to his attention to ordinary life. Jesus continues the tradition of the Hebrew Bible by taking images and figures for God and God's action among us from the stock-in-trade of daily existence. God's life among us is not expressed in abstract plans, or even in the language of the royal courts, but in parenting, baking, farming, and so forth. The commonplace images reflect Jesus' insistence on God's presence in all creation, and in the most fundamental human relationships and responses. A preacher who forgets this fundamental rooting of Jesus' revelation of God runs the risk of distorting or obliterating the good news.

THE PARABLES OF JESUS

Jesus' parables are an important focus for an exploration of his use of imagery, because in them he directly addresses the issue of God's realm on earth, and of everyone's relation to that reality.[8] In their very ordinariness, these stories are intended to grasp the hearer directly, to alert the hearer to God's activity already present among us and also yet to come—in its fullness in the world—and to invite and challenge the listener to respond to this new awareness.

In this process Jesus holds together two complex elements of the revelatory reality of images: the image connects the hearer's ordinary world with the divine and at the same time opens up this world to unexpected manifestations of God.

For instance, in Mark 4:26-29, Jesus compares the reign of God to a farmer who scatters seed in a field. All the time the seed sprouts and grows, whether the farmer is asleep or awake. The farmer neither knows how it happens nor controls it. But still the harvest matures and is reaped. Every hearer would recognize the ordinary situation of agriculture, which even with today's more sophisticated knowledge and technology evokes some of the same feelings as were felt by the first-century farmer. The farmer does what is humanly possible, but the actual growth and maturation of the crop is dependent on forces humans at best can only partly control. The harvest occurs only in small measure because of something the farmer does. The activity of a far greater power is required for the growth of crops and the harvest that results.

Every hearer of the parable could identify with the farmer, but at the same time each would be pulled into a world view in which everything we do, all our works of goodness and labors for God, is like the farmer's effort—important and necessary, but only the occasion for divine power to bring forth a reality far beyond our capacity. The inbreaking of God's reign and presence among us are gift and grace, not human work. It is unpredictable and unexpected, even as we hope for and expect it. God changes the world; we have only a small but necessary role.

Consider also Luke 15, the familiar parable of the prodigal son, in which Jesus confronts us with the same dynamic of the familiar setting and the unexpected activity of God. The parable's final words add a question for us. The story is familiar, one which each hearer has participated in, either in her or his own family, or with others. We the hearers are a part of the tale as it unfolds here and now. We may see ourselves in the prodigal, but we are also invited to look at ourselves as the older brother, the righteous one who remains faithful but will not rejoice at the reconciliation of the whole family.

And when Jesus ends the story, it remains unfinished. We do not know what the elder son said or did, and we do not know how the younger son lived out his repentance. The story is not finished because we are part of it. The surprise of the parable is not simply in God's unexpected action among us, but rather our astonishment at finding ourselves in the middle of the action, invited to react. The images of Jesus' parables do not lie before us to be examined, but pull us into the dynamic of the story, and call us to respond.[9]

3
Preaching the Image:
How Can the Words Work?

After pondering the question of why preachers today must be open to the vital importance of imagery in biblically based, contemporary preaching, a fundamental question emerges clearly to us: What shall we do? We have explored the importance of imagery from the perspective of many contemporary disciplines, and we have inquired into the biblical perspective and imagery. We accept with enthusiasm the importance of imagery for the warp and woof of our preaching, for imagery as a way of focusing our sermons. Our spoken words in the sermon are the primary medium for the imagery that centers our preaching, that gives it life and coherence. And now what?

Recently many works have appeared about storytelling or narrative preaching and about art and images in preaching.[1] All of them have struggled with some of the most thrilling and frustrating aspects of this new approach to preaching. Because all of these approaches are so rooted in the aesthetic sensibilities of the preacher, this style of preaching would at first seem easier caught than taught. How can anyone set out guidelines and other suggestions about a kind of preaching that wells up so directly from the imagination and the heart of the preacher?

This dilemma is real and unavoidable. But at the same time those of us who teach preaching are faced with the daily issue: we are employed to teach, to attempt to communicate directly to the student of preaching something about the various ways of growing in wisdom about the task of proclamation of the word. As members of congregations, we have been subjected to earnest, newly minted preachers reading us *The Velveteen Rabbit* at Sunday liturgy, assuming that we would automatically be flooded with spiritual insight. Both as preachers and as members of the congregation, we also have been cheered and delighted by sermons that "work," that express simply and movingly

God's Word to us. We also have experienced frustration and have felt limited when we have tried to analyze why and how a particular sermon was effective. Sometimes our congregations did not feel our words work and they could not tell us why. We have felt baffled by our own efforts and those of others.

As is true about all activities involving the aesthetic sensibilities of the human person, we cannot reduce preaching and imagery to a rational-cognitive exercise. The contemporary understanding of the human mind warns us against regarding logic and reason as the most important and convincing mode of discourse in religion (or in almost anything else). At the same time, our approach also requires us to affirm a cognitive dimension to images and imagery. In images, our feelings and our thoughts unite; they find form and expression. As noted before, images have both affective and cognitive dimensions. When we ask questions about how we may best preach in and with imagery, we engage in an enterprise that integrates the intellect and the emotions.

Because images bear within themselves such complex human freight, embracing heart and mind, a discussion about imagery used in the sermon must attend to the role both of affect and intellect. If either is missing or shortchanged, then the imagery used in a sermon is inadequate for its preaching work. Because preaching focused in imagery incorporates all dimensions of the human person, we can and must identify how the cognitive and affective meet, relate, and work together in images. We know that only if all the dimensions of the mind work together will our preaching be effective in communicating the Gospel to the whole person. We also need to be alert to the fact that what works for the preacher may not always effectively communicate to all among the preacher's congregation. Ultimately, no approach is foolproof and guaranteed to reach everyone perfectly every time. But we can be more precise and intentional in our efforts to communicate effectively the good news of God's grace active among us.

THE IMAGE AND THE SERMON

As we noted in chapter 1, the term "imagery" refers to the whole sensory dimension of the sermon, not just an image or picture. Thus the imagery in a sermon encompasses the verbal descriptions and evocations of the visual, tactile, auditory, and all other dimensions of the physical world. In any sermon, or in any human communication, one cannot simply reproduce the physical world in one-to-one correspondence. One identifies certain aspects that seem either most important, most noticeable, or most linked to what one is trying to express. Those dimensions of the visible world one sketches evoke in the hearer something of the vision the preacher wants to communicate. Nor are all details of equal importance; some may be downright distracting, and not to be used in a given sermon.[2]

For example, if we were preaching about the Good Shepherd and wanted people to feel something of the dangers of the Judean desert, we might want to spend some time and effort describing how dry the sands and rocks are, how little water there is, how hard it is to find water, and how short a time it takes for a waterless sheep to die. All of these details communicate rather directly to our awareness of how much the sheep need the shepherd. However, if we go off into a discussion of the flora and fauna of the desert, a detailed description of Judean wolves, the boring diet of the shepherds, and the strange and dangerous people one finds in the desert, we will be in danger of distracting people from the relationship between the Good Shepherd and the sheep, the focus of our image.

Normally we will want to make one particular image central; other images either will clarify or support it. Sometimes another major image will appear along with or supporting the primary image in a sermon. Sometimes these other images find their places as deliberate contrasts to the primary image. For instance, one might preach a sermon about God as rock in which the sands of a beach express the inadequacies and insecurities of our own ambitions and efforts to determine the course of our life. Other images supporting and expanding the range of the biblical imagery may be used. An example might be in a sermon on the rich man (Dives) and Lazarus, in which the contrast between the poverty of Lazarus and the wealth of Dives is supported by an exploration of the sights and smells of contemporary poverty and wealth in Manhattan. The key to the integrity of the sermon is the underlying cognitive and affective unity of its imagery.

In the process of creating a sermon, one will find a vast array of biblical and modern images suggested by the biblical material. The preacher will engage in much praying, listening, and experimenting with various images before the primary image is chosen and the work of shaping the sermon is finished. But before that work can constructively begin, the preacher needs to have some sense of what sort of imagery is most appropriate to contemporary preaching.

No hard and fast rules can or should be made about how to identify helpful images and construct a sermon from those images, but the following guidelines should be generally helpful. The first step, of course, is prayerfully and thoughtfully to explore the Scripture readings assigned for the service of which the sermon is a part. One needs to ask a wide range of questions for reflection about the situation. What kind of liturgical service is it? (Eucharist? Morning prayer? Evening prayer? Community interdenominational service?) Is it a Sunday service or on another day or occasion? During what liturgical season does it occur? What will be the liturgical setting? Who are the people (laity and clergy) participating? What is the relationship between the congregation and the wider community of which it is a part?

Depending on the time and place, the congregation, and the shape and tone of the service, a particular image may emerge from the Scripture and beg to be the center of the sermon. For instance, if I were preparing a sermon for a small rural congregation in midsummer of 1988, during the period of drought and crop loss, I would attend very carefully to the agricultural imagery in the Scripture. For Proper 11 of Year B in the Episcopal lectionary, the Gospel appointed is Mark 6:30-44. After Jesus and his disciples have withdrawn to pray, they are followed by crowds who seek his teaching. Jesus is moved by pity for them, and then feeds the crowd of five thousand. For people necessarily preoccupied with their own crop losses, the image of Jesus feeding a multitude can be both attractive and a reminder of a physical abundance they do not have. In the context of the Eucharist, I might first bring the congregation into the scene of need, hunger, and physical and psychic distress. Jesus' loaf of bread reminds us of the bread God gives us to provide us with a very particular kind of nourishment. Such a focus connects people to familiar images, but also opens up an awareness of the different kind of feeding Jesus came to do for us. At this initial stage, when the Scriptures are speaking to us about the sermon itself, we ought to explore some nuances of the image and how it will shape and offer meaning in the sermon.

Congruence

Images communicate because they express a likeness between the concrete, physical reality and an invisible but equally significant reality. G. B. Caird discusses this quality of imagery, noting that this sort of explanation is based on similitude. Much of our learning, he points out, depends on the ability to move from the known to the unknown by way of comparison—this object I know is like this reality I do not know but wish to understand.

Such comparisons can fail, Caird notes, if the known image is not actually known to the audience. But more importantly, images will miscommunicate if the point of comparison is misunderstood or wrongly identified.[3] The preacher cannot ensure that everyone will always grasp every comparison. However, one can try to clarify the image and that which it is showing the hearer. Sometimes the images are bound by culture and time, and the preacher needs to attend to a presentation of the image so that the listeners will understand the image on which the comparison is based. (For example, to grasp the chariot image Plato uses in the Phaedrus, one must have a basic notion of the workings of a chariot before proceeding to the anthropological explanation.) But whether they are related to specific cultures or to nature, the preacher must be conscious of the relationship between the image and the world into which it pulls us, and the way in which everything in the pre-sentation of the image contributes to pointing out the connection.

The imagery of the sermon needs to be consistent with and expressive of the religious experience, ideas, and feeling to be conveyed. "The Lord is my light and my salvation; whom then shall I fear?" asks the psalmist (Ps. 27:1). As I allow the image of light to enter my awareness, I see, where only darkness was before. Light is the medium that enables us to see. If I am lying or sitting in the dark, I am wrapped in my own dreams and perceptions. I might be asleep and dreaming pleasantly or with nightmares, or I might be awake but unable to perceive even my own body, much less the furniture, people around me, or whatever might surround me. I might enjoy the stillness and silence and absence of visual contact with my surroundings. I might be fearful and uncertain, listening to the cry of unknown birds and animals, or hiding in my bedroom, alarmed by unfamiliar noises that might come from burglars downstairs.

In the midst of my darkness light dawns. That which was uncertain, perhaps menacing, often unknown, is open and clear to me. I can see what is around me; I am able to identify my own body, where it is and how it relates to that which is around it. The hidden and suspicious are made known, clear, and open. In this clarity I am able to identify where I am, what surrounds me, and how to respond. My happiness and confidence rise because I visually connect with the world about me, can perceive and assess it, respond to it as it is—not only as my imagination depicts it—and can feel more certain about the actions I will take. Light gives me the security to say with the psalmist, "Weeping may endure for the night, but joy returns with the dawn" (Ps. 30:5).

To acclaim God as my light portrays God as the one who illumines and connects me to the world. God shows me what the world is like, where safety and danger are, where the sources of pleasure and pain are, where I am in relation to myself and to everything else. God graciously decides to do this for me, and thus the notion of God as light expresses an intimacy and nurturing of God for us. God freely chooses to become the medium through which reality is interpreted and given to us, the one who offers us the world and shows us where we are in relationship to it. In God we see who and what we are; without God we are as helpless and unaware as the proverbial seeker for a black cat in a dark room.

The preacher who selects light as a focal image will be consciously and directly aware of the congruence between the image of light and the centrality of God for the believer's life. Using the image effectively necessitates the preacher's showing the connection between light's action and God's illuminating activity. The sensory power of light implies that God not only offers us perspective on the world but also evokes joy in us as we enter this relationship to the world. Any sermon in which light is a central image will necessarily center itself on the intimate care of God who acts as our light, the new vision God gives, and the joy and sense of safety evoked in us.

Of course these are not the only possible interpretations of God as light. But the integrity of any sermon depends on its capacity both to let the cognitive dimension of the image shine through and also to be sure that whatever is articulated is congruent with the image. For instance, a sermon about God as my light and my help, which focused on God as the one who judges the world and who shows us all our sins, might be right and true, and might also be appropriate for some uses of light. But such an interpretation is not congruent with the dominant biblical image of light, and confuses the ordinary and most fundamental significance of light. When such shifts in imagery are made, as in John 9:39, Jesus uses this image of light as judgment with a clear dependence on and reference to the basic comparison between light and God's helping action in such texts as Psalm 26. When preaching about such texts and using light imagery, one needs to be aware of the fundamental congruence, and be sure that one's preaching communicates the basic relationship, and the way Jesus' use of the image modifies and shifts it.

Commonality

The most effective imagery in preaching is directly and immediately familiar to the hearer. In our consideration of the impact of the parables, we noted that much of their power depends on their very ordinariness. The reign of God is depicted as a pearl of great price, as yeast in the dough, as a crop growing in the field. God is also a shepherd, a housewife, a king, a mother hen. All of these figures were common to the lives of the people of biblical times, and the capacity of these images to evoke response from people depends on that very familiarity and ordinary quality.

Almost everyone of Jesus' hearers had seen a mother hen breathlessly pursuing her chickens around the yard at the first sign of danger, trying to collect each of them under her wings to protect them. Thus each of Jesus' hearers could imagine the gracious concern of God, who would go to such great and undignified pains to gather an ungrateful people in order to nurture and protect them. Listeners also saw themselves in the foolish chicks, who scatter and elude the care of the hen, rather than seeking the only safety possible for them.

The "punch" delivered by the image in part depended on its being accessible in ordinary life. In *The Parables of the Kingdom* C. H. Dodd insists on the ordinariness of the images in the parable; the same could be said of any image used in sermons:

> At its simplest the parable is a metaphor or simile drawn from nature or common life, arresting the hearer by its vividness or strangeness, and leaving the mind in sufficient doubt about its precise application to tease it into active thought.[4]

A relationship between God and the people could be directly and plainly apprehended because everyone had a firm grasp of the image itself. Any image we use in preaching will lose much of its power if it is not also common to our hearers. This causes no insignificant problem for preachers.

Many of the biblical images are not common to our world. We do not live in a primarily agrarian society in the ancient Near East. If we begin with the most accessible aspects of biblical imagery, however, we discover that many biblical images are in whole or in part available directly to us today. For instance, most of the natural phenomena such as light, dark, and rain, are also familiar to us. Parental imagery is in part for us what it was in ancient Israel. God is sometimes imagined as friend, which is the same and perhaps even more central to us today as then.

Some images are not directly a part of our experience, but in part available and can be presented "in context" as a part of the sermon itself. For instance, many people in American congregations have never seen either a shepherd or a live sheep. They probably have, however, seen television programs or films about shepherds, and have some secondhand knowledge about shepherds and sheep. Given this common awareness, and some solid knowledge of biblical times and customs, a preacher can present a vivid word picture of a shepherd to a congregation in so clear and strong a way that people can sense just what a shepherd is and how sheep and shepherds relate. Through carefully shaped presentations, the Biblical image can be made accessible to a congregation in such a way that the religious impact of the image will be clear and vital.

Or, to illumine the biblical images, the preacher may choose to select a contemporary image serving some of the same functions for us as a corresponding image in biblical times. For instance, instead of a shepherd, the contemporary preacher might focus on the scout leader who guides the troupe over unfamiliar territory, or the block leader in the city who tries to ensure that everyone in the neighborhood receives what he or she needs from the city government. Most of the time in the sermon the preacher will want to develop the contemporary image thoroughly and make a clear connection with the biblical image.

No matter what image the preacher uses, she or he must attend to the congregation's awareness of it as an ordinary part of their lives. An image that is not somehow rooted in people's experience cannot effectively convey much about God's own belonging in their everyday lives.

Multidimensionality

Multidimensionality, the rich ability of images to sustain many meanings, includes two related elements. The first is the capacity of the image to communicate to various dimensions of the human person. The strongest and most effective images are those bearing many sorts of meaning, appealing to the intellectual, affective, and sensory aspects of the person. The second is the image's ability to contain many new meanings and referents, all of which can be seen to be connected to the several aspects of reality, all bound up in the one image.[5]

At the beginning and the end are the senses. If the physical image is not strongly and vividly present to the hearer, then all the other dimensions of meaning will be lost. If the preacher starts a sermon by acclaiming God as a rock, then the congregation needs to see the rock. Is it a big rock, or a pebble? Is it a strong rock, a boulder in the field, or does it rise unexpectedly and overwhelmingly from the yellow plains of the desert? Is the rock massive, smooth, and worn, a shelter from the heat of the sun and a wall to lean against, or is it steep and sharp, hard to climb because it trips and tears you, but offers you the safety of Mesada when you have climbed it? The congregation should feel the unyielding power of the rock, the heat of the sun reflecting off it, and rejoice in its protective height.

If the preacher would take us to Mount Zion, to the rock on which the temple stood, we would stand before the steep road leading up to its heights, climb amid the rocks and the dust, until reaching the top of the hill where the sun gleams on the high, white walls around the temple. We would feel the sand and grit between our toes, and sense the unyielding hardness of the rock beneath us. Our hand would reach out to the side of the path, where the pebbles and sharp stones broken from the rocky hill cut and bruise us as we trudge on toward the top, from which we can see all Jerusalem. The preacher needs to lead the congregation on this sort of verbal sensory journey.

If our senses are not fully active and involved so that the image becomes a vital part of our reality, then nothing else of the sermon will remain with us either. Sometimes the image will slip past and be forgotten, or perhaps bits and pieces of it will remain, with no connection with anything else. The preacher may find herself or himself in the situation of the college professor visiting with a former student. "Professor," said the alum, "I will never forget the day you stood on top of your desk and crowed like a rooster. But I have forgotten what you were trying to tell us."

The image is central to the sermon, but the preacher needs to be aware of and to shape the ways it flows forth to affect the other dimensions of the person. Occasionally an image can merely be presented, and because of the particular readiness of the community and the specific liturgical context, interpretation would be superfluous.

Such situations are rare. Usually various elements of meaning need to be made specific in some way. For example, what is the affective significance of the image of God as rock?

Cannot such an image inspire awe at the immensity of the great rock towering over the tiny and fragile human being who wishes to climb it? Is a rock not a place where one can feel secure, safe from the enemy and able to rest, to survey the land, to overcome attacks and develop one's own life within the protection of the rock?

The most effective feelings are conveyed not by telling people what they ought to feel or think, but by letting the image evoke the thought and feeling. For instance, how weak is the feeling conveyed by the statement: "As I rested in the shade of the great rock in the desert, I felt secure and safe from the heat of the desert, and was reminded of how God keeps me safe from temptation and the dangers around me." More effective is an approach that offers this kind of observation: "When I stood atop the rough granite hill, I looked out over the village where are my home and shop, my friends and family, and these few who wish evil against me. I remembered the ones who have come and gone from the town, the making and breaking of friendships, and the illness and death that parted me from my own youngest child. Beneath my foot a fallen branch from a fir tree cracked, and I felt below it the unyielding granite that cradled me and my fading dreams, as it had held uncountable generations before me. This rock upheld me, as an even greater rock sustained me, the hill, the village, the land beyond, and all of our hopes and confusions. And for a moment I knew I was safe on a rock that would keep me forever."

And if God as a rock evokes certain feelings in me, such an image also provokes my intellect to assert some truths I have perceived about God. If, for example, my sermon centers on God as rock, then one of the theological issues raised is God's dependability. If I stand on a rock, then I experience something about its possibilities and its limits. I can stand on a rock for security, but eventually even the rock will crumble, and might even crush me or someone beneath in a rock slide. The very stable rock is beneath its surface appearance a swirling mass of energy. If I speak of God as rock, then I am focusing on one aspect of God, the divine dependability, God's capacity to provide a place for me that I can see and be aware of what is about me.

God does not offer me physical safety or the power to conquer my enemies as an ancient warrior did by standing high on a rock. God the rock does guarantee presence to me: no matter what happens, God is faithful and present, and will not go away, any more than the mountain will get up and leave. Not only is God faithful in this sense, but if I am willing to enter into a relationship with God, God will offer me a place of perspective from which I can stand and confront my enemies, knowing that whatever they may do to me now, God's faithful love will endure and triumph. And as much as I share in God's faithful life, I am safe from the power of ultimate destruction. God as rock is a sign and symbol of God's enduring love and protection, and calls us to respond in confidence to the divine trustworthiness. Thus the image of "rock" for God provides something universal in its connection between our human experience and hopes, and our interaction with God.

The helpful image in preaching is one that resonates with all aspects of the person, that consistently and coherently appeals to all of the person—senses, emotions, intellect. The multiple dimensions of the image are equally important, and all dimensions of the person are necessary participants in the personal hearing and receiving of the Word. The multidimensionality of the image provides rich reservoirs of meaning for preacher and hearer. The more effective the preaching, the more it is aware of and addresses all of these elements of the human person in the way the image is shaped and structured in the sermon.

Appeal

If we want people to listen, our sermons must appeal to them. Appeal does not necessarily mean like or agree with, but appeal does involve immediate identification with some aspect or quality that I am happy, ready, or able to find in myself. On an elementary level, this need for some sort of appeal in the image is why I would never try to preach a sermon about how God is like a gila monster, a rock slide, or a dried-up stream (Jer. 14:18). There are indeed traces of God in all creation, and every image can reveal something about God and humanity. But one has to hunt hard in these images to find something appealing that will attract hearers and not just repel them. The sermon is not the place to do that.

Sometimes scriptural imagery confronts us directly with this issue. One winter at a local church, I was leading a discussion group about imagery in the Psalms. My last session had centered on Psalm 68, in which the primary image is of God as warrior, conquering lord of the heavens and the earth. During the class, even though everyone had been enthusiastically participating in previous sessions, people were reticent, somewhat resistant, and finally the study ended in a whimper.

As I muttered over my own failure, people's lack of cooperation, and the gloomy grey weather, a friend reminded me of the obvious, which I had overlooked. The parish is in the midst of Manhattan's East Village, in an area filled with drug traffic, much violence, and large numbers of homeless people. Many residents were feeling pushed out of the neighborhood by rising prices, and many parishioners were trying to nurture a community in a hostile environment. Most of the members of the congregation were heavily committed to working for international peace and justice issues, as well as local community development and welfare.

God as a warrior was antithetical to everything for which most members of this congregation lived and died. I used the image in an adult education class, and unwittingly learned an unplanned lesson. As a result of that experience, I decided I probably would never again use this biblical image in preaching to this congregation or perhaps any. Even though we could explain the sources of the image, its context, the good reasons for it to be in the Scriptures, nevertheless the emotional havoc it wrought was too great. The image was so overwhelmingly repelling to that particular congregation that the hearers' energy would have focused on interpreting and struggling with the image, rather than attending to the Word proclaimed in it. Sometimes it might be important to center on an image that repels a particular congregation. But the preacher needs to be aware that the sermon that day needs to be a reinterpretation and reclaiming of that image. Then perhaps the next sermon can center on letting the word and wisdom of God emerge from that image for the congregation.

The church has always been concerned with the effects that the images it uses have on the hearer. For instance, Pauline theology in the New Testament focuses on the saving work of God in Christ in the cross and resurrection of Jesus (e.g., 1 Cor. 1:17-31, Gal. 6: 14-15). However, in the extant archaeological remains from the late first century into the fourth century, the cross is a minor theme, infrequent in art. Instead the good shepherd, the teacher, and the fish are all central pictures. In preaching, the image of the cross is found as a cosmic symbol of reunification of the four elements and directions of the world. Where one might expect to find an image of the cross with the crucified and/or risen Jesus, as in Melito of Sardis's Paschal sermon, the central image is Jesus as paschal lamb and the cross is a minor illustration. The biblical image of the cross of Jesus is converted to a universal sign, often devoid of its concrete reference to Jesus and his crucifixion. Other images carried that religious weight in preaching and art. It appears that Roman sensibilities were so offended and disturbed that the church did not make the crucifixion a central visual or verbal image until well into the fourth century. The church preached Jesus' death and resurrection, but other images besides the cross were used to convey the depths of Jesus' self-giving love.[6]

 Has the shape and tone of the Gospel varied somewhat throughout history because of the different images used? Of course. But among these different themes, the Gospel still engages people in God's action among them. Different images take center stage in the preaching in any given era. Not all images can be given equal weight to all periods in all cultures. The preacher's challenge is to ensure that important aspects of God's self-revelation to us are not hidden because we don't want to bother discerning some of the complexity of the good news we are called to preach, and to find images that bear the gospel.

For instance, when I recognize that I cannot use the image of God as warrior with a particular congregation, I find that in Psalm 68 other related images appear besides God as warrior: rider of the clouds, rider of the heavens, father of orphans, defender of widows, Savior. Each of these bears upon God's sovereignty and redemptive activity. I will still be able to preach the good news of God's reign in the world and exercise of power on our behalf. In important religious ways these images are related to the warrior image, as their presence in the Psalms assures us. But because they are not directly connected with force, violence, or the destruction of others, people could be more open to hear them and the good news proclaimed by them.

Open-ended

One of the greatest joys of a good image is that it always has more grace and truth hiding in it, ready to emerge to meet us when we seek for it. C. H. Dodd writes about a parable's ability to leave the mind in enough doubt as a "precise application to tease it into active thought." Images tease us into active thought because they are always susceptible of surprises and new interpretations. A good image contains unending potential for God's revealing Word to be known to us. No matter how often we preach on or consider it, the image always bears more riches.

It is open-ended in the sense that great art or a beautiful sunset is always unfinished in relationship to the viewer. No matter how often you behold it, more remains to disclosed.

Several years ago I attended a "contemporary service" in a mainline Protestant church. After the first hymn came the opening prayer: "O God of affirmative action and positive vibes, . . ." We were in deep trouble. This prayer conjures up images of an affable, well-disposed new age deity, supportive of everyone's equal opportunity and wanting everyone to be happy and cheerful. The image itself is flat and one-dimensional. No hidden riches lurk here; the intellectual content is plain but little more is evoked or given.

John Donahue and Frederick Borsch explore this aspect of images in the parables in light of Dodd's comments about teasing us into active thought. They identify this as the parable's polyvalence, its capacity to be legitimately interpreted in different ways.[7] Donahue uses as an example Matthew's use of the parable of the lost sheep (Matt. 18:12-14) to encourage church leaders to care for the weak of the community, whereas Luke (Luke 15:4–7) employs the parable to justify Jesus' mission to the lost outside the community. Each of these interpretations is quite different, but each is anchored firmly in the parable itself. Good images always have this capacity.

In John's Gospel, Jesus says to the disciples at the Last Supper: "You are my friends if you do what I command you. I shall no longer call you servants, because a servant does not know his master's business. I call you friends because I have made known to you everything I have learnt from my Father." (John 15:14-15) Jesus contrasts two images describing two different relations with God: Master/servant, and Friend/friend.

Both images are rich and have borne much weight from the whole biblical tradition. Each stresses different aspects of the human relationship possible with God. The Friend/friend image is of particular importance in the Scriptures, because it focuses on an extraordinary relationship of equality possible for the believer. Jesus, who is sent by God, calls the believers his friends, a status they did not have before. Jesus does not call them God's friends, but his. Jesus stands before the disciples as one who is of them, yet more than they, because he has been sent by God, whom he calls Father, to reveal God's love to the world. He is the intermediary, who makes them his equals, rather than his inferiors and servants.

As the Christian tradition developed, the notion of friendship with God also grew. A theological jump was made: If Jesus came from God and was God's equal, and if Jesus was our equal as a human being, and had called us his friends, then through Jesus we had become God's friends. And so the imagery of God as friend became an important part of Christian devotion. God was present and struggling with the believer, not as master or warrior, or lord of the heavens, but in an intimate relationship in which the believer is invited to share in God's own life.[8]

All of these interpretations can be derived from the image of friend, but the journey marks a great journey from a realm in which God is a sovereign over all, to a world in which this same God is also one who is present to people and shares their experiences. Not only has more been discovered about God's self-giving to us, but the image has offered glimpses of God's reality that have transformed Christian theology and devotion.

Over the centuries the image of God as friend has conveyed to Christians a sense of God's intimacy, saving help, challenge to the future, and love in the presence. God as friend is a strong and open-ended image, which has offered new and surprising developments to Christians over the centuries. A preacher whose proclamation of the Gospel comes in such images offers the congregation means for God's revelation to continue and grow in them.

4
Prayer:
The Preacher's Bread

Every lecture or book about preaching admonishes the preacher to pray as an essential part of sermon preparation. How could anyone dispute such advice? If preaching is proclaiming the Word of God, a part of the liturgical prayer of the church, the preacher must be always rooted, grounded, and living in prayer. But the language of obligation and of necessity leads us to suspect that prayer is a penitential exercise or a requirement to be fulfilled. In his collection of poems about the church, *The Temple*, the seventeenth-century poet George Herbert wrote of prayer: "Prayer the Churches banquet, Angels age . . . Exalted Manna, gladness of the best." Piling image upon image, Herbert pictures prayer as the Christian's nourishment, that which sustains us because it is "God's breath, . . . the soul's blood." The Christian needs prayer because it is essential to us, because it is God's life in us, giving us "softness, and peace and joy, and love, and blisse."[1]

Every preacher needs to nourish himself or herself in prayer, because prayer is our contact with God. How can preaching have other roots than life in and of God? Otherwise the one who proclaims the Word runs the risk of being like Paul's "sounding brass and tinkling cymbal," making a lovely noise, but with no substance behind the sound, shaping beautiful utterances about a reality she or he understands only at second or third remove.

Every preacher needs prayer as nourishment, because prayer is the normal way God's life enters us. All one's learning, reflection, awareness of the world, and capacity to speak effectively and appealingly, all find focus and reality in relationship with the living God who is being proclaimed. Prayer is not an address to God; it is listening and speaking with God, receiving from and offering to God. Prayer sustains our life because it is the gift of God's own life to us. Prayer is the preacher's daily bread.

In a little book of reflections about the Psalms, *Bread in the Wilderness*, Thomas Merton compares the prayer of the Psalms to "bread, miraculously supplied by Christ, to feed those who have followed him into the wilderness."[2] The reality of God's life nourishes us in the Psalms and in the Eucharist because it is the Word of God that feeds us. When the preacher prays, she or he reaches toward that Word in confidence that it is manna in the desert, that it will feed us no matter how desolate or isolated our circumstances.

The preacher's life of prayer is a necessary prerequisite to preaching, but it provides more than raw material and background information for preaching, as though prayer gives the preacher a product to be added to the other ingredients, which can all be combined so that a sermon will emerge. Prayer itself has a movement, a dynamic, emerging out of our contact with God and helping shape the sermon itself.

PRAYING THE SCRIPTURES

We can name as many different ways to pray as there are people, but it is possible to identify certain basic elements in praying that may be most helpful for the preacher.[3] We humans pray in many different ways, from the simplest "O God, help!" to elaborate, hours-long liturgies. Some of our formulaic prayers demand little intellectual concentration from us, while profound contemplation may take us on a journey from intense reflection to submerging of consciousness in the presence of a greater reality. All Christians at different times and stages of their lives may engage in any of these and other sorts of prayer.

For the preacher, biblically rooted prayer is most directly linked to the proclaiming of the Word. Not only does such prayer respond to and speak in and through a dialogue with Scripture, but such a living prayer also immerses us in a movement of the human encounter with God. Such prayer is helpful not only in the way all prayer is useful and nourishing, but it also moves us to ask questions, participate in the various hopes and conflicts of the human condition, and receive God's response as offered to us in Scripture itself, the basis of our preaching.

In a very helpful little book intended for laity and clergy alike, Elizabeth Canham addresses some of the basic questions we twentieth-century Christians face in praying the Bible. Often laity who have heard about biblical criticism are frightened away because they don't think they know enough to read the Bible responsibly, so they drop either the Bible or criticism. Clergy, most often the preachers, know so much about the technical aspects of biblical scholarship (although perhaps very little about its use) that they sometimes give up all attempt to pray the Scriptures devotionally. Canham seeks to help both clergy and laity find a way to pray the Bible in an informed and responsible way.

Such an approach is essential to the preacher, who while praying is at the same time aware of exegetical and historical questions about the Scripture. This Scripture is itself the focus of prayer and preaching. How can we find the living God through the words of the text heard critically and prayed devoutly? Canham offers some practical and helpful suggestions.

Following the direction in which Canham points, the preacher who would pray the Scripture with devotion and learning with heart and mind, can discern a basic process to prepare for the event of preaching. One over-arching rule is quite clear: prayer and preaching thrive best as integrated parts of a disciplined interior life. Any preacher who dashes into the sacristy on Saturday afternoon to hunt up the readings for tomorrow scarcely has time, much less the disposition, for thoughtful and prayerful work with the Scriptures for the day. The way one approaches preparation for preaching is an expression of the integrity and discipline (or lack of such) in one's whole life.

We gain our nourishment through a disciplined life in which we take time to let ourselves live in and pray the Scriptures as though we are a part of them. Henry Mitchell relates how the black preaching tradition has encouraged this kind of prayerful life:

> The story must be internalized in the preacher, peopled by characters he [sic] has known for years and for whom he has such deep feelings that he can authentically recreate the action and communicate the experience.[5]

Although imagination is essential to prayer, it is the imagination of openness in mind and heart to the God revealed in the story of Scripture.

Early in the process of preparing the readings for preaching, one needs carefully to read and prepare an exegesis of the texts, as much in the original languages as possible, and with as much awareness as one can muster. Then one reads with more search for focus. One needs to explore the readings with a clear and searching attention, as early as possible before one preaches, so that one may grow and seek for awareness. What are the human situations, questions, tensions, or concerns that emerge from the reading and address one? Who are the characters, how do they interact, and what is the plot of the action? What are the tensions and resolutions? What are the places that "itch," where the conflict presses the preacher, where the word seems puzzling, confusing, challenging, requiring a deeper dialogue?

Up to this time the tenor of the investigation might be somewhat detached and intellectual, a look at the text. Prayer unquestionably introduces one into a face-to-face dialogue. To pray the Scriptures is to enter into them in the faith that they are the expressions of a world in which God was and is active, and that they are a means through which God here and now communicates with us. The preacher who prays the biblical text uses her or his critical knowledge to open up a world in which God speaks with our ancestors in the faith, and invites us into the dialogue. In and through the intellect and the imagination, the preacher believes, the Holy Spirit speaks to us.

This next stage, that of prayerful entrance into the Scripture, requires the preacher to identify the Scripture that focuses what one wants to preach about. At this one has some awareness of what issue, question, or tension provides a likely impetus for a possible sermon. For example, I was to preach in my parish church (Christ and St. Stephen's in Manhattan) on the Sunday closest to Sept. 28. In the three-year lectionary cycle we use in the Episcopal church, these are the texts for Proper 21 of the season after Pentecost, Lectionary Cycle C. The readings appointed are Amos 6:1-7, Ps. 146, 1 Tim. 6:11-19, and Luke 16:19-31.

Luke's Gospel lured me from the very beginning. Powerful as the other texts are, its complexity, open-ended plot, and vivid sketches powerfully attracted me. Because we are in mid-town Manhattan, on the west side, in the middle of a neighborhood that is rapidly gentrifying, I felt challenged by the issues of power, wealth, and responsibility, which appear so dramatically in the story. With all the homeless and indigent, are we like the rich man in the story? Is there any sense in which the character of Lazarus speaks to us, except in condemnation? Does Jesus offer any message of hope, in his own context or in ours?

After I had done some exegetical work with Luke's text, I knew that this Gospel spoke to the complex situation of poverty, wealth, and responsibility in which we live. Now that I had a general sense of the direction in which I wanted the sermon preparation to move, I needed to learn more from the Gospel about poverty and wealth, how these conditions affect people, how my world relates to the biblical world, if it does, and what Jesus' comments mean to us today. I knew that to gain access to this world I needed prayerfully to enter it to understand the people and to hear the Word proclaimed through the text.

THE SHAPE OF THE ENCOUNTER

Depending on many circumstances, including one's own condition of readiness, sometimes one can just walk into a text and everything emerges clearly. But usually one is helped by a method to get one through the dry times and to help one in moments that seem utterly devoid of inspiration. Many different approaches are possible, but the one that seems to offer the best combination of direction and opportunity for free play is a loose version of the Ignatian method of meditation.[6]

John Booty notes the influence of this style of meditation on late sixteenth- and seventeenth-century theology. A. G. Dickens, Louis Bouyer, and other historians have noted the general lines of connection linking Catholic and Protestant spiritualities in their formative years after the Reformation.[3] These historical studies show the preacher how in an earlier period a particular form of mediative prayer was commonly used by Catholics and Protestants to help them in that prayer which is preaching. Some of the preaching that emerged from that period is among the most vital and exciting in the Anglican tradition, and suggests sources of life for our preaching today.

This particular approach allows much use of imagination, sensory awareness, intellectual insight and reflection, affective response, and quiet listening for God's Word. It requires activity and waiting, and provides structure and guidance, facilitating an encounter with the divine without forcing any particular element. A busy preacher will also learn that this method lends itself well to a schedule. Usually one would spend from a half-hour to an hour engaged in such meditation at any one time.

IGNATIAN PRAYER

In the sixteenth century, Ignatius of Loyola devised his approach to prayer on the basis of his own experience of conversion and relationship with God, and throughout his life refined his writing about methods of prayer.[4] In recent years, theologians, historians, and pastors have rediscovered great value in Ignatius's disciplined approach to prayer.[5] In the *Exercises* Ignatius recommends three modes of prayer. The variations depend on one basic approach, which was sometimes presented in great detail and sometimes in a simpler way.

The *Exercises* are designed to lead a person to a more serious commitment to a life in Christ. Ignatius asks the retreatant to begin with a consideration of the mystery of salvation, then of Christ's kingdom and how one shares in and serves Christ. The type of prayer described here is meditation. The *Exercises* asks the retreatant to meditate daily in order to encounter Christ and to be moved to respond to God's call to her or him. Ignatius suggests methods of prayer and meditation in the *Exercises*. The next few pages identify the major steps in Ignatian prayer.

Scripture is the usual beginning point for one's prayer. Normally, in order to be prepared, one reads over the passage (e.g., Luke 1:39-56) the night before and decides what particular aspect of the story one wishes to meditate on. Even if the next day's prayer should develop in a completely different direction, it is important that the person praying should prepare with as much effort as possible.

The next day, when beginning the meditation the person praying begs from God the grace to be "fully oriented in witness and worship" of God. After this introductory prayer, which reminds us of who we are and what we are trying to open ourselves to in prayer, the person begins the so-called first prelude, the relation to physical time and place in which the biblical event takes place. So, for instance, if one were praying about the visitation of Mary to Elizabeth, one would try to place oneself in first century Palestine, at this time in Mary's life. Ignatius explicitly encourages one to use one's imagination. Thus one should try to picture the house, the roads, the rocky hills, the dangers of a woman travelling at this time in her pregnancy.

In the second prelude one asks God for what will help one pray in this place. One might, for instance, pray for the faith to rejoice with Mary at this difficult time in her life with God, and to share her excitement as she sees the fulfillment of God's promises through her cooperation with God. After this one enters into the event, applying one's memory, mind, and will. This part of the prayer is generally the longest and most detailed time. For instance, if one gives an hour to the prayer, this part could well take more than forty or forty-five minutes.

As one enters into this part of the prayer, full exercise of our senses and our imagination is essential to bring us as living participants into the biblical scene. One way to share in the event about which one is praying is to imagine oneself as a bystander in the event. For instance, one might be a servant in Elizabeth and Zachary's household who has met Mary on the way and escorted her into the family's courtyard. We see and hear the events, see the difficulties Mary has undergone as well as the joy she brings with her. We behold the meeting of the two women, their enthusiasm and fear, their determination.

We can speak to them, ask them what they have thought or felt, how God has acted in their lives, how much of a surprise the voice of God was for them, how they responded, what their hopes and fears have been. We give ourselves time to become a part of their world, to let them take on their own life, and share it with us.

Not only do we ask and listen, we reflect on what we hear. What, for instance, does it mean that "the child in her womb leapt for joy"? Although my prayer is not a theology lesson, still, I need to have some understanding of what the evangelist meant, and how I can interpret that now. What are the links between the child's and the mother's joy? What sort of joy do they share? How does their joy relate to any joy I might share?

For Ignatius, the human will involves decision making. Consequently, my prayer necessarily includes not only imagination and intellect, but also will. That is, how does my encounter with these persons— Mary, Elizabeth, perhaps also with God who is present—move me? What does it show me about myself that I would like to change? To strengthen? To be firm and constant in? Is there something I want to do as a result of what I have seen and heard?

Ignatius believed firmly that although prayer required imagination, which enabled one to leave oneself open to an encounter with Jesus and other figures in the Gospels, this prayer was not simply an imaginative exercise. Prayer is encounter with God, involving effort and talk. Equally important is listening to the voice of God expressed through these biblical figures. They use the voice and the expressions of one's own imagination and one's own world, but at the same time God's voice is also speaking. Listening is essential to prayer. Deeply embedded in the process of prayer, especially as one begins to conclude, is the centrality of quiet, calm attentiveness to the voice of God speaking in the time of prayer.

We who so often think of prayer as "speaking to God" sometimes forget that listening is even more important than our talking. We listen in faith that God is really present and will communicate with us. Of course we will have to try to discern and interpret God's Word from our imaginative clothing of it. Perhaps for us moderns it is more essential first to be confident that God is present and will speak to us, and only then to worry about how to assess and interpret God's Word to us. Ignatius has guidelines for discernment and understanding of God's Word to us in prayer (for instance, God's Word would never contradict Scripture by leading us to despair of divine mercy). Before discerning what God has spoken to us or shown us from our own imaginings and fantasies, or even from destructive thoughts, we must first listen with attention and faith to what God gives us through our prayer. Sometimes we will see pictures, hear words, recall quotations, or become aware of fresh relevance and insight in something that seemed familiar. Frequently as we pray to Jesus we will hear him speak to us. Whatever the form is, we attend to it assuming God's Word will come to us in this dialogue of prayer.

We will often experience our listening and speaking with God as an interchange, a conversation in which God communicates to us and we explore more fully the impact of God's Word for our life. Ignatius writes that the dialogue can be that between a friend and a friend, or a superior and subordinate. It can ask questions, apologize, consult, or collaborate. No matter what the tone or direction, our prayer helps us explore more deeply the ways in which God is involved in our life, and we with God.

This prayer, Ignatius insists, ought to finish with specific connections between God's Word to us emerging from our scripturally based prayer and our life and activities. Our prayer will invite us to some specific change or resolution for our life. Our prayer is not an abstract reflection on some abstruse or entertaining theme, but an exploration with God of our relationship, and the way my life reflects God's love and call for me. For instance, meditating on the visit of Mary to Elizabeth, I might be most attracted by Mary's joy in sharing the good news of God's kindness to her. As I speak with her, I discover how much I fear sharing my joy even with those who are most eager to hear my experience of God. I resolve to identify a person whom I feel certain will welcome my story about God's involvement in my life. I ask for the grace to share my story with this person, and to seek with her or him for ways I can grow in my willingness and ability to spread to others the good I have received from God.

In Ignatius's view, prayer always connects the biblical word, the active Word of God to us through the Scripture, with our life. From his perspective prayer is action oriented, because prayer is the articulation of a process in which we live our lives in increasingly closer interconnection with God. Prayer is eminently practical.[10]

Through this approach Ignatius promotes a sensory-based, image-focused prayer, which provides the center from which the affective and cognitive dimensions move and to which they return. For a preacher who wants to pray and preach with the whole of human personhood, this style of prayer provides a direct and helpful dynamic for the shaping of a sermon. How might this approach be applied in preparing a sermon?

AN IGNATIAN APPROACH

To illustrate, let me take my experience with the passage from Luke (16:19-31) about the rich man and Lazarus. Previously to my praying with the passage, I did my scholarly critical and exegetical work with the text. Then the day or evening before my prayer, I carefully read and reread the text, to fix it in my mind. The next day, to begin, I decided to spend a few minutes in immediate preparation. I need to be comfortable, but not inviting a nap, in a place and time where I am unlikely to be disturbed. I also want to be aware of the people among whom I will be preaching—who and what they are, their challenges and questions. I invite them to come along with me, as friends and companions who are also a part of me. I also consciously place myself in God's presence, reminding myself that I am trying both to reach toward and to hear and receive God. I come to God with my doubts and fears, but also my desire to hear God's word spoken to me that I may let it live in my life and in my words. After these preparations, I begin to meditate.

First I try to set the stage, to imagine myself there in a city in first-century Israel, perhaps in Jerusalem, in front of the home of a very rich man. I want to see and feel the strong stones, to watch the hot sun shining off their white surfaces, to see the lizards sunning on the rocks. I see the small knot of the poor and distressed, who clamor at the gate for alms every time someone goes in or out. From within I hear the sound of laughter and music, and leave the dust and sweat of the road to cool myself in the chambers within, where the family and friends wear fine-dyed linen, and even the servants look sleek and prosperous. On the table before me I see mounds of dates, almonds, and figs, joints of lamb, piles of flat bread, and flasks of wine so abundant they seem endless.

I begin to enter more fully into this scene. Two people in particular catch my eye. They seem to embody the two extremes. In the house I see the wealthy head of the family. He is so identified with his wealth that Jerome transforms his designation as a rich man into his name, and the Latin Vulgate's term *Dives*, the rich man, became his proper name in early English language translations and preaching. Because I want a name for him, I too have called him Dives. He is quiet, well-mannered, courteous, and honest to his acquaintances. He entertains well, dresses the part, and appears to enjoy being rich. But he seems not to have enjoyed giving anything away to those who were not his own kind, well-connected as was he.

My vision of the rich man, so prosperous and noted for his conspicuous consumption, contrasts vividly with the emaciated beggar at his gate, Lazarus, who is like an embodiment of destitution. He is covered from sores, perhaps from disease, but more probably from the effects of malnutrition, dirt, and parasites. Although he wants food from the rich man, he doesn't seem to have the energy even to beg. And as he sprawls there hopelessly, slowly starving, only dogs (unclean scavengers from the Jewish perspective) lick his sores. Lazarus has sunk as low in the human social scale as one can, and appears only to want to be fed with what fell from the rich man's table. But no one would give him anything, so he only lies silently at the gate.

The contrasting picture of these two human beings, who would have crossed paths several times a day as Dives strode in and out of his sturdy and well-tended gate, draws me further into the story. I want to stop the action there at the gate. "Look," I want to shout at Dives. "Look over there by your beautiful, expensive gate. See that pile of rags? There is a person underneath. He is smelly and unpleasant, but he is also starving here right in front of you. Do something."

Lazarus, whose only scrap of human dignity seems to be that he has a name, frustrates me too. "Damn it, do something; don't just lie there and starve. Make him feel guilty. Breathe your decay in his face. Beat on one of his dogs. Curse, howl, protest." But Lazarus lies there as Dives rushes on.

But these are two humans of flesh and blood. Neither Dives nor Lazarus is an evil person, seeking to hurt others. Why do they ignore each other? I must ask them each that question, and I must ask myself, for a bit of each of them lives in me.

How many times have I passed someone on the street who has asked me for something? I could give, but I usually don't. Sometimes I smell alcohol, sometimes I don't. I get tired of listening to tales of woe, some real and some entertaining fantasy, and I shut my heart and refuse to see the other person. The effort is too painful, difficult, and time-consuming.

If I refuse to give directly, then I know I need to give faithfully and generously to others who can help. But I don't really give commensurately with my refusal to give to people on the streets. I feel it to be too much trouble, and besides, I have worked hard to be a self-supporting citizen. I don't need to beg and I don't depend on others.

There, of course, is the rub. That grubby person on the corner differs from me by only a few modest turns of chance. In fact, that person differs so little from me that I cannot bear to face our proximity. What if I were to lose my job? What if I drank to obliterate all the pain of the human condition? What if I had not graduated from college? What if I had not received that offer to go overseas? What if friends had not said, "It can be different, you can make a life with a future"? What if? There I am, sitting on the corner too. Not only have I met that person, I am that person. And I fear myself there.

So I listen as Dives and Lazarus speak to me of fears and hopes fulfilled and shattered. How have they each been locked into worlds that do not meet? How has Dives grown so obsessed with himself that he pays no attention to the most fundamental religious laws of responsibility for the poor? What has smashed Lazarus and sapped his energy so that he can do nothing for himself, neither beg nor demand what is due him under the Law? And I listen to myself in both of these people, to the deep forces in my own heart that resonate and respond to them. I am trapped with them in distress, fear, anxiety, and callous avoidance.

Before God I bring this pain and conflict. I listen for God's discernment to be made known to me. How does God see it? But more compellingly, what can God do in us, in me? Are we stuck, so that Dives and Lazarus are utterly separated, eternally and irrevocably? Could it be different? Is there any hope of reconciliation?

Silence and listening are vital here. Most of us, especially clergy, talk far too much, and assume much too easily that we know what God wants. Let us listen. I am quiet, trying to leave aside all of my preconceptions simply to hear what God will offer. If I am quiet and patient, eventually I hear some word from God, sometimes mixed in with all sorts of other stuff, but usually clearly enough for me to recognize God's word expressed not only to me, but to all to whom I am called to preach.

We humans, Dives and Lazarus alike, can look at each other and try to understand and help each other. I can find in myself something of Dives and something of Lazarus, and I can hear and acknowledge this shared humanity. I can experience, in the Word of God and in the Eucharist, God's gathering us together, in which I share a common meal and a common life with Dives and Lazarus. We are already one in God. Particularly because I will be preaching in a Eucharist, I am acutely aware of the shared nourishment and shared lives to which we are invited at the Lord's Supper, and the contrast of this sharing with Dives and Lazarus's encounter. If I let myself feel and know that, I will want to be different. I will feel myself incomplete and torn if I do not act to bring reconciliation between rich and poor, in myself and in society.

As we are bound and nourished in Jesus' Eucharistic life shared with one another, I know that I am called to share this life with others, in word and deed. This sharing involves every aspect of my life—time, goods, abilities, and money. And so I hear God asking me to let my interior self be changed by God's gracious life shared with me. I also know that such interior change demands action of me.

What can I do to let my life express God's life itself shared with me, binding me with both Dives and Lazarus? I can stop thinking pious thoughts every time I meet an able-bodied person panhandling me on the streets. If I don't give money to that person, then I am still called to give. For instance, each time I am stopped on the street, I can set aside a quarter for a specific program to aid the homeless or to donate to an advocacy agency for those who are being displaced from their dwellings. And what about the humanity of Lazarus? Can I not find for myself a way to respond to an individual who seems to have no urge at all for "self-improvement" as a human person who might have very good reasons for feeling this way? How can I reach out to speak the word of hope and open up the vision of a better present and future?

Can I name one way to transform my fury at the rich, who seem oblivious to the needs of others, into a sympathy for their apparent need to hide from such a demanding world, and into a way of communicating to them specific ways to extend themselves to other human beings who are their sisters and brothers? And so on.

I ask for myself the one question that seems most crucial now. When I meet Lazarus and Dives, in the parable, in the parish, and around the city, I beg God that I may meet them with empathy and love. May I respond to them with grateful respect for God's work in them, and with the courage to invite them to encounter one another as sisters and brothers in Christ.

At the conclusion of my prayer, as at the beginning, I pray that God will transform me in the power of the Spirit who dwells in us. I have moved into the Scriptures to hear God's Word addressing me, and now I go into the world to live the Word I have heard. I thank God for what I have heard and received, and ask for the love and the courage to live out God's Word in my life.

When one first begins to practice this kind of meditation, it may be helpful to make a few notes about how one began the prayer, the way one imagined the biblical episode, the dialogue that emerged from this encounter, and the prayer for grace one was finally moved to make. Some sort of journal or notebook will be indispensable. In time, the preacher may find writing down notes from one's prayer less necessary. In any case, it is important only that one remember what happened in meditation, just as one remembers an important conversation one has had with someone one loves. Notes and sketches will serve as a reminder of the living encounter with God in prayer.

Such prayer cannot be an infrequent activity. We will recognize this as we become more accustomed to it. We will not be physically fit if we exercise once a month or once a week. We cannot know a person intimately if our conversations are infrequent or only held to get something. If we wish to enter into the mystery of God's life with us, our prayer will be a daily activity, as regular as eating, sleeping, or talking with friends and family. In such a context, the prayer that shapes our sermons will be a natural, easy part of our lives. Our sermons will ring with the conviction of one who speaks of a reality in which she or he partakes.

No one method of prayer will be always useful or forever the most appropriate. Just as one will discover different ways to converse with a friend, various approaches to prayer will grow. One will find new and exciting links between one's prayer and one's preaching. Most of us, however, will find it helpful to have some shape and form for prayer to guide us on good and bad days, and to help us when we are feeling uninspired. Ignatius's method is especially helpful to the preacher because it provides a sturdy structure that at the same time is flexible and open. Because it focuses us in prayer through imagery, it is especially suitable in shaping image-centered preaching, as we will explore more thoroughly in the next chapter.

5
Shaping the Sermon

Prayer that is a living encounter with God ought not to be shut outside the door when we begin to draw our sermon together and let it take shape for worship. In this chapter we explore the ways in which the prayerful meeting with Christ, and with the world he leads us into, give form and direction to the sermon to be preached. As an example, I will show how meditation focusing on a particular gospel (the story of Dives and Lazarus) gives birth to a sermon for the Sunday Eucharist at a particular parish.

DYNAMICS OF PRAYER

Out of the encounter with God in prayer, the sermon itself rises and takes shape. The kind of scripturally based prayer we have explored does not take the preacher into the Scripture primarily to find a thesis or to evaluate possible ideas critically. This prayer guides the preacher into and through an encounter with Christ, and with the world of Scripture. The preacher prays in faith to a living Christ. In and through Christ, all whom we meet in the Scripture still live. The preacher lives and prays in faith and openness to Christ and in solidarity with all those who live in Christ.

Such prayer opens the preacher to the freedom of a living encounter with God. Thus one cannot say beforehand, "I will find or learn or feel this or that." One can only trust that from the meeting, grace will burst forth and God's Word will be made known. But such a living encounter also leads us to meet Christ in his world, and as in all meetings, certain patterns of action emerge to shape our behavior and prepare us to receive all we can from God's activity with us.

The shape and movement of this prayer does not, however, cease with the time of prayer, but continues directly into the form of the sermon. The prayer in which Ignatius guides us as we encounter God in Christ in the Scriptures moves us in a dynamic way that combines structure and freedom. In a methodical process we imaginatively place ourselves in the context in which God is made known to us in the Scriptures. Then we speak and listen to Christ and the other persons in the biblical event to help us discern how through this Word from God we are being invited to a transformation by grace. The movement of this sort of prayer is set up as an exploration of people and situations, dialogue, and response. Our encounter with God always connects us with this world, and invites us to change ourselves that we may be more fully Christ's friends and disciples in the world. No one form of preaching is necessitated by such a method of prayer, but some approaches are more congenial than others. This chapter explores structure I have found particularly helpful.

SHAPE AND MOVEMENT
IN THE SERMON

During two thousand years of Christian preaching, people have explored different styles of preaching and various theories of rhetoric. In this latter part of the twentieth century, our culture has become more aware of the limits of syllogisms and logic. Thus it comes as no surprise, in perusing contemporary literature about preaching, to discover that preachers are increasingly less interested in forms of the sermon based on the three-point logical syllogism promoted by Broadus and other standard nineteenth- and twentieth-century writers about preaching.[1]

Eugene Lowrie has suggested a model many of us had inchoately been searching for in our preaching.[2] He rightly asserts that the sermon is a narrative, rather than a logical construction composed of a pile of conceptual bricks. As with any other narrative, it has a plot, with certain necessary twists.

Lowrie identifies these stages: upsetting the equilibrium, analyzing the discrepancy, disclosing the clue to resolution, anticipating the consequences, and experiencing the Gospel. After establishing the tension, the preacher discloses the clue to resolving the pain and points to the Gospel resolution.

Lowrie's third stage, that of disclosure, is the key—where the unbearable tension breaks open and the possibility of healing is suggested. He is correct, and has identified that element of any good sermon must contain: the upsetting of my expectation and the healing of a tension I feel deep within myself.

We have already noted that imagery is not merely a static picture, but the total sensory content of an event, episode, or picture. Imagery is the physical component of story, narrative, and parable. Such imagery is effective because it is multidimensional and open-ended. Tension and unsettledness lurk in all good imagery. It is what it appears to be, but it is more, and it pulls the viewer into itself, so that it might be revelatory and transform the beholder. For instance, the image of rock is rich for the preacher because rock is more than a substance that feels and looks hard and grey.

The biblical imagery of rock contains within itself an element of revelation. In 2 Tim. 3:17 we read that "all Scripture is inspired by God and useful for refuting error, for guiding people's lives, and teaching them to be upright." To a modern ear these words sound moralistic and combative, as indeed they are. But from the context of conflict in the early church, the author of Timothy conveys a conviction that is strong in the church's appreciation of the Scriptures—they are *for us*. Sometimes the gift is direct; other times the encounter confronts us with a past vision of God or relations with God we no longer share. But in any case, in our encounter with the Scripture, we meet God, sharing an experience that brought our ancestors faith, light, and hope.

Imagery is a fundamental dimension of scriptural discourse. Biblical imagery does not simply exist on a page, to be reconstructed or re-captured verbally or visually. One may analyze or probe the imagery, but the imagery itself (as an expression of God's self-disclosure to us, when we respond to it in prayer and preaching) grasps us and pulls us into the human encounter with God. Our bodies, minds, and spirits as a whole are brought into contact with God and God's dialogue with humanity. John Calvin wrote of the Holy Spirit's role in our apprehension of the meaning of Scripture:

> The Word will not find acceptance in men's [sic] hearts before it is sealed by the inward testimony of the Spirit. The same Spirit who has spoken through the mouths of the prophets must penetrate into our hearts to persuade.[3]

Scripture—which speaks to us, which is our prayer—is God's conversation with us, directed to the heart, not just the intellect. God addresses us as beings who perceive, feel, and act. Consequently, God's address to us is persuasive, not just informative. God's self-revealing is intended to move and involve us in a life with God. From this perspective, any living encounter with imagery springing from the Scripture is revelatory and thus involves a plot. As one perceives the image and allows it to affect one, tension, change, and transformation are involved.

For instance, if I prayerfully read Psalm 40, with its imagery of God as rock, I certainly see and feel the physical reality of rock. But the physical dimension does not exist in itself, in a vacuum. It expresses something of the divine to me through these senses. The hardness of rock is palpable, but in the psalm it thrusts in front of me the fragility of my own flesh, the danger threatening to overwhelm me, and the stability and strength of God who alone can save me. The imagery evokes from me the tension between my own helplessness and fear and the deliverance I hope for from God. The image of God as rock suggests to me the possibility of a transformation in me through the help of a God who offers me rocklike stability.

Lowrie's work centers on narrative preaching. Because of the nature of the encounter of the hearer of a sermon with its imagery, the same basic movement is involved. I would rework Lowrie's description of plot somewhat, and identify three crucial movements for any sermon.

A sermon should begin by introducing tension and unresolved conflict. Sometimes this tension will be an externally observable conflict. For instance, in John 18:33-40, Pilate and Jesus face each other as opponents. Jesus is a troublesome rabbi whom Pilate has to judge, and in Pilate Jesus confronts the powers of this world who silence and thwart him without even understanding what he is preaching. Other times the tension will be internal, as in Matt. 26:69-75, when Peter, who has adamantly denied Jesus three times, realizes his own weakness and disloyalty, and breaks down in tears.

Unresolved conflict at the beginning of the sermon catches all of the unresolved conflict in us—the regrets, uncertainty, incompleteness, questioning, pains, and longings. A sermon begins by calling out to everything in us that is unresolved, and that sees the conflict in the world about us. The preacher begins by evoking from us our own desire to seek healing and transformation for our broken and conflicted human condition.

In the central movement of the sermon, preacher and congregation are caught up in the tension, identify with it, explore it, and can imagine no way out. Into this heightened awareness, anxiety, and uncertainty, a word of hope breaks. Peter is not condemned to sit forever at the gate weeping for his betrayal; Jesus' death and resurrection give him reconciliation and hope. We are not abandoned forever hanging in the inadequacy of our efforts and blindness of our lives. The good news proclaims hope.

The sermon's resolution draws together the tension, its roots and ramifications for life, and the possibilities for hope God offers us. How does Scripture show us God's transforming grace at work in our lives to change our pain into rejoicing? Jesus does not leave Peter forever mourning his infidelity at the gate; Christ's resurrection offers a chastened Peter a place as shepherd among forgiven sinners. We who acknowledge before God our own weakness and lack of faith see in Peter how God's forgiveness and grace can offer us greater compassion and strength than we could ever have on our own. The risen Jesus offers us hope that we can live faithfully amidst our own weakness.

The imagery that is the center and focus of a sermon bears in itself this dynamic. Imagery contains its own plot, its own fundamental movement leading the hearer of the sermon from the tension of a challenged, troubled, conflicted self, more deeply into the life with God that offers hope and transformation. From that perspective, imagery and narrative are complementary dimensions of human reflection on and testimony to our life with God.

I have already written (in chapter 4) about a form of prayer that is particularly helpful in appropriating biblical stories and images for preaching. The basic movement of the sermon flows directly from this kind of prayer, at the same time that this movement reassesses and reshapes the prayer for the event of preaching in public worship itself. This prayer leads one into the Scripture, and helps one explore the characters, the events, the specific images, and the general values and certain truths. It helps one attend to the nuances of tensions, conflicts, and the human predicament at the foundation of every story of the Scripture. In praying the Scripture one finds oneself in it, identifying with and exploring the depth of the conflict. As one prays and explores, the Scriptures themselves reveal that resolution is possible. The Scriptures point to hope and suggest what the promised transformation of life might look like.

SAMPLE STRUCTURES

Here are two examples of what such a sermon structure might look like. The first can be illustrated using the story in Luke 16:19-31 of the rich man and Lazarus; both examples center in the imagery of the story and intend to draw the parallel between the biblical world and our own. They differ in the form by which they structure the connections between the biblical imagery and the realm of the contemporary believer.

The first approach draws the connections between biblical and contemporary worlds at each major movement in the sermon. The basic flow of the sermon construction is simple, consisting of three stages. At each stage one encounters the tension between Dives and Lazarus and the tension among and within us.

A First Shape for a Sermon: Luke 16:19-31

1. *Dives and Lazarus:* We begin by exploring the world of these two persons, their appearances and their surroundings. What were their internal moods and motivations? The major issue emerging at the beginning is the separation between the two by their wealth. Lazarus lies at the gate, isolated from all human contact. Dives appears unwilling or unable to "meet" and respond to Lazarus as the Law calls him to, at least through alms-giving.

The preacher asks how our world is related to Dives and Lazarus's world. As a point of comparison that seems to resonate with the biblical situation, I cite an experience I had on a trip to Dallas, in which I spent some time at a conference in a luxury hotel and then back in the rundown neighborhood where I grew up. At this time I encountered the same sort of separation of rich and poor as was lived by Lazarus and Dives.

2. *Exploring the roots of tension:* Why are the two persons, these representatives of rich and poor, so separated from each other, alienated and hostile? What is the root of the animosity? Dives and Lazarus are the symbol of the alienation of rich and poor, their perpetual separation, which seems to be hopelessly fixed.

In Bernanos's novel, *Diary of a Country Priest,* I found a contemporary vision of why people create an unbridgeable gap between rich and poor. Bernanos's observations illumine both the biblical picture of the separated Dives and Lazarus, and the contemporary chasm between rich and poor. In this perspective the preacher sees that resolution of the conflict can only come through God's deliverance, which alone can break down the barriers we set up.

3. *How the gospel offers hope of resolving the conflict by overcoming the alienation:* The only hope of deliverance for Dives and Lazarus would have been a different ending for the story. What if they could have encountered each other's needs and exercised a capacity to help each other? They might have allowed themselves to be human beings together before God.

The preacher needs to ask what the resolution of the alienation between rich and poor might look like for us. Here the Eucharist can serve as an image of encounter and healing. The sermon needs to explore some of the specific manifestations of healing the division between rich and poor. The hope and the challenge of the sermon is that we are free, as Dives and Lazarus once were, either to meet and be healed in Christ, or to remain alienated.

These suggestions for the shape of the sermon pick up on what is, to my imagination, one of the most poignant scenes of the whole story: Lazarus lives at the very gate of the rich man's house and the rich man never even sees him. Jesus does not reprove Dives for not helping far-off needy people, or for defrauding his colleagues, or for maltreating his servants. Here right in front of Dives was an obvious subject for the relief of the poor to which the Law of Moses called the rich. Helping Lazarus was not a religious option for Dives; it was a command. Instead of giving Lazarus money, food, or medical help, or even thinking about offering him some help, Dives did not even notice Lazarus. Dives cut the poor beggar out of his conscious awareness and did not see in him a human being for whom he had some responsibility. The chasm between Lazarus in heaven and Dives in hell is only the eternal counterpart of the gap Dives has himself made by ignoring Lazarus.

The *image* of the unbridgeable gap between Dives and Lazarus focuses the story. It becomes the visual center and is the structural clue to interpreting the story. It also provides a way to show the transformation made possible through the power of the gospel, which enables people to encounter and respond to one another. The unity of the imagery is also maintained by the preacher's ability to move back and forth from the biblical to the contemporary scene, reinforcing the connection between the scriptural and the contemporary worlds.

In this approach, we follow the movement of the encounter (or lack of it) between Dives and Lazarus, connecting it at each stage with contemporary life: First, we see the tension between wealth and poverty. Second, the conflict develops until it is plain that no human person or resource is able to bridge the gap. Third, we suggest the possibility of the resolution through an encounter with each other and healing that only God's grace can bring about.

At each stage, both the biblical and contemporary lives are explored, and the exploration and movement in each are developed together. This approach works best when the connection between the biblical and the contemporary world seems clear and straightforward, demanding a minimum of explanation of the relationship.

A Second Shape for a Sermon: Psalm 40

Here is a second possible structure, the major movement in a sermon that explored the image of God as rock in Psalm 40. In the first part of the sermon the dynamic of the biblical image is explored, beginning with the clarification of the tension implicit in the image, moving to the exploration of the tension and conflict until its roots are exposed and the hope for resolution is identified, and continuing with some exploration of the resolution and transformation of the conflict through God's action. The second half of the sermon takes the same movement and applies it to the contemporary life of the believer. In effect, in the first half the preacher explores the biblical image, and in the second part, which is parallel to the first, contemporary life.

The Psalmist's Conflict. 1. The preacher begins with the contrast between the psalmist who is in the pit and God who is firm and steady rock. The external conflict in the psalm revolves around the struggle between the psalmist and his enemies; the internal tension explores the fear produced by the psalmist's awareness of the sins that take away his confidence.

The psalmist's perilous situation is contrasted with the stability of God as rock. The preacher might explore what rock means in this environment and religious world, including all the possible meanings— from the rock as a specific place in the desert on which one might be safe in battle, to the rock of Mount Zion as the cosmic foundation God has set against chaos.

2. The exploration of the tension involves exposure of the psalmist's weakness before his enemies and guilt before God. The question to be explored revolves around the motivation that leads the psalmist to cry out to God the rock for deliverance in spite of sins and loss of confidence.

God's response points us to hope. God comes into the pit and lifts the psalmist out. (The preacher will want to be aware of the ways the image becomes very plastic and moves about in "unnatural" ways.) Often in the Scriptures an image of God will "shatter" and open up new depths of meaning through this sort of change.

3. The third stage is to explore what the transformation looks like for the psalmist, how secure the psalmist feels being on the rock, safe against enemies. What is the transformed relationship to God the rock like?

Our Relationship to God as Rock.   This is the changing point in the sermon, when the biblical imagery reveals itself as "for me," as true for the contemporary believer and not just the psalmist. Here the preacher will explore what the biblical image means in the lives of the hearers in the congregation.

1. The preacher asks: What it is like to live in chaos, to feel as though you are always treading water in a river with no bottom? How are we like the psalmist who feels threatened by enemies without and uncertainty within? How do we feel the need for a rock to uphold us, and what does it feel like to experience the absence of God as our rock?

2. What is it like to turn to God for help, to call God to give foundation and certainty to our lives? We want what constantly eludes us, and the more desperately we seek to make our own security, we feel its inadequacy and fragility. We cannot even guarantee the order of our own lives, much less the world. So we can either choose chaos or seek the God who can give firm stability to our lives. We experience the psalmist's struggle as our own, and like the psalmist, can find no other hope than God to support us.

3. What will it look and feel like to be confident in God, to be secure on a rock that cannot be destroyed and that is at the foundation of everything else? The preacher explores the kind of life we can lead if we are founded in God as our rock. What might our lives become if God's gracious love were the firm foundation for our lives and deeds?

This second approach is most helpful when the biblical imagery needs some development, and when it may not be clear to the hearer how the movement from the identification of the tension contained in the image moves into its healing and resolution. Sometimes the preacher may feel the need to give more sustained explanation; other times she or he may want to be certain that the congregation has a clear grasp of the meaning of the biblical image and its significance in the Scripture. Especially if the preacher is directly dependent on a text that is either not familiar to the hearer or is commonly misunderstood, the preacher may want to present first the whole biblical dynamic without other reference. With the biblical development plainly in view, the preacher may then directly confront the contemporary situation.

The preacher may imagine other movements for the sermon, or develop them through further reflection. These two examples I have suggested provide clear alternatives, focus directly on the Scripture, and prepare one to speak directly to the situation of the hearers in their communities. The preacher needs to feel free to seek various shapes and forms for the sermon. In this quest, the preacher also needs to be responsive to the requirements and desires of the congregation, and to the integrity of the scriptural text. To show what I think this process of shaping a sermon might look like, I will present one sermon; it explores imagery and typifies the movement I am suggesting.

6
Preaching on the Rich Man and Lazarus

In spite of having exerted ourselves mightily to prepare, all preachers are constantly confronted with a fundamentally haunting question: How will the sermon work? Will people be moved by God's Word spoken through it? Will the images be clearly presented and evoke a response from the hearers consonant with the Scripture? Does the sermon help people encounter God as known to us through Christ?

Ultimately one should not worry too much about the reception the sermon will receive, although many of us will secretly desire ahead of time to know people's responses. Just as a plant sprouts from a seed, or an adult emerges from childhood, a sermon will grow as a result of the preparation process. Its growth continues as it is delivered to the congregation, where it acts as a "living Word" for the people.

I have already suggested how prayerful preaching might be done about Jesus' parable of Dives and Lazarus in Luke's Gospel, and a sermon sketch developed in chapter 5 about that passage. I preached a sermon about this text at Christ and St. Stephen's Episcopal Church in Manhattan in September of 1986. Although any of the texts appointed in the lectionary for the day (Year C, the Sunday closest to Sept. 28) might have served as a focus for a compelling sermon, I decided to use Luke's Gospel.

Luke's telling of Jesus' parable of the rich man and Lazarus presents the hearer with powerful imagery inviting one into a world of sharp contrasts between rich and poor. The story shows us a man offered a choice between serving God through obedience to the Law of Moses or yielding to evil that casts one into Hades. The visual and tactile imagery centers on the rich man (*Dives* in Latin, a description that became his name in Western church tradition) dressed in silk, and feasting at teeming tables, and on Lazarus, so poor and ill that only the dogs came to lick his sores.

This biblical scene, featuring these two vivid figures who see but do not encounter one another, evokes in the hearer an " 'intricate dynamic pattern' of feeling."[1] In this case, the story centers on the juxtaposition of these two contrasting persons, one lying silently by the gate, and the other constantly bustling in and out of his house, yet never noticing the beggar who was so distressed. Jesus fixes this contrast as the center and the tension of the story. It is the pivot on which everything moves. From this focus emerges the discomfort, insight, and challenge.

Dives and Lazarus exist in the same plane, inhabit the same place, but never intersect. Dives ensures that by refusing to see, to acknowledge Lazarus, by not allowing himself to help or even greet a human being like himself who is physically right before him. Dives denies humanity to Lazarus by not even admitting his existence. Dives does not recoil in horror from Lazarus or sputter out his contempt; he refuses to see Lazarus as anything more than part of the background scenery of Dives's privileged life.

The texture and fabric of the imagery, with its dynamic revelatory movement when Dives begs Abraham for some contact with the now blessed Lazarus, is rich. With this imagery, the preacher seeks to evoke a response of emotional affinity, insight, and decision from the hearer. Because one seeks to evoke varied sensations, and a range of cognitive and affective reactions and actions in the sermon, there may be more than one picture or image in a sermon.

For instance, in this sermon we see a picture of Dives and Lazarus at Dives's mansion; we also see pictures of a luxury hotel and a rundown neighborhood in Dallas. But one image (in this case, that of Dives and Lazarus at the gate) will usually provide the basic structure about which all the elements in the sermon revolve. The connections will sometimes be directly obvious. Other times, as in the chorale, they will seem to contrast, and the unity will emerge later. A congregation can enjoy much play within the imagery of the sermon, if the preacher will provide resolution and harmony at the conclusion. These contrasts are most likely to work if the preacher has captured the imagery of the story in a way that contains the seeds for such a resolution.

I chose the Gospel text for this sermon because I personally find the contrast between these two figures powerful and fascinating. Because the story is unfinished, as in all parables, the hearer is left uncertain about the future, eager to know what will happen to the rich man's family, delighted that finally Lazarus is receiving his reward. Yet the listener also wonders if some way can be found to cross over the pit of hell in which the rich man is submerged. If Abraham can talk across this great divide, is not some resolution possible? Is it too late for Dives to repent? For his family? For all people trapped in their wealth like Dives?

The main characters also appeal to me because neither seems to me especially admirable or damnable. Jesus depicts ordinary people at opposite ends of the social-economic scale. Each of them to some extent is caught in a system he cannot control. Yet Jesus also suggests that some choice is possible, even when one cannot change everything to be as perfect as one wants.

I decided to introduce parallel imagery, which originated in my experience of having grown up in Dallas, a city of economic extremes. I wanted to sketch the aspect of first-century life Jesus centered on, and then to portray the same dynamic in a contemporary situation with which I was familiar, and into which I could invite my hearers to enter. I was fascinated by the contrast and the similarities between Dallas and first-century Palestine. Despite the profound differences between the physical appearances of the first- and the twentieth-century cities, the same fundamental sorts of relations between rich and poor prevail.

It seemed to me that if both the hearers and the preacher could enter into the dynamics of the contrasts and connections between that first-century world and a twentieth-century scene that was similar to but not identical with our own, we might learn something about God's Word for our own situation. How are we who are well-off in this world like Dives? What does God call us to do? What about those of us who are in Lazarus's condition today? What is God's Word to us? And how does God invite us to relate to one another?

In 1983 I had preached a sermon on the same Gospel text at the General Theological Seminary, in New York City, where I teach. That sermon raised some of the same questions and explored some possible responses. I was preoccupied with my development of the contrast between Lazarus and Dives and I was sure that there was little or no good news to be heard. So in 1986 when the opportunity to preach about the same propers arose again, I was glad for the chance to reconsider and rework my whole approach.

During my time at Christ and St. Stephen's, I had become more aware of ways we were trying to respond to the challenges of the poverty outside and inside the doors of our church. Our parish has tried to be responsible in responding to needs of parishioners and of others, but as is often true in busy parishes, it was often hard for parishioners to be engaged with the people we met in various projects. Giving and receiving of goods and services were important, but how could we become more conscious of each other's human worth, and of the ways in which we are interdependent with one another? Because our parish is eucharistically centered, I wanted to raise the question of the role of the Eucharist and our encounter with Christ in the sacrament and the encounters between the rich and poor who gather around the altar in our city.

I decided to use my own experience of returning home to visit Dallas as the foil to the biblical story. Part of my reason for employing it was the depth of my experience. Certainly I was affected by the experience, but I also found it to be a remarkable counterpart to the contrast between Dives and Lazarus. Perhaps the Dallas setting was so inviting because the contrast between rich and poor is not only extreme, but is also new, widespread, and unapologetic. When I revisited Dallas I found that it still was not wrestling with issues of social and economic responsibility in the community. From that perspective, the city was very much on that parabolic edge referred to in Luke's Gospel. It needed to choose whether rich and poor would be separated by a great chasm, or whether somehow rich and poor can meet, so that some healing of their wounds can begin.

The image I focused on was the gap between Dives and Lazarus. The images I encountered in Dallas arose in a similar social predicament as in the Lucan story. These pictures gave the hearers a recognizable counterpart to the first-century setting. Centering on the image of the gap between Dives and Lazarus, I decided to focus on the movement from unresolved tension of the separation between poor and rich to our recognition of why we have constructed the gap and are ourselves unable to bridge it. The only possible resolution of the tension and conflict is through acceptance of God's grace in overcoming the chasm between Dives and Lazarus, rich and poor. In context, the image of the eucharistic meal pointed to resolution through the grace of God.

My hope was to bring the congregation on a journey in which we moved from the apparently hopeless situation of Dives and Lazarus, and the wealth and poverty of Dallas (both situations in which haves and have-nots were inevitably and permanently divided), to a condition in which some hope could be affirmed. The sermon's movement was from division to at least the beginnings of unity, from an isolation we create and enforce to the community only God can give. As we let ourselves enter into the transformation God offers, as pictured in the eucharistic table, we are enabled to see how our interpersonal relationships in God imply changes in the way we share our goods with each other.

SERMON

"Dives in Dallas"
A sermon preached on Sept. 28, 1986
in Christ and St. Stephen's Episcopal Church
New York, NY

"There was a rich man, who was clothed in purple and fine linen." He was an honest, upstanding member of the community, enjoying his diligently earned wealth. He dressed and ate according to his station in life, and lived in the palatial home appropriate to his wealth. In the tradition of the Latin church he has come to be called Dives, "the rich one," as his proper name. He was the very model of a productive citizen.[2]

If we had been able to interview him as he strode purposefully from his home to the marketplace, he probably would have identified himself as happy, satisfied with his life and the way the world had treated him. He worked hard and played hard. He fulfilled his social obligations, paid his temple tax, was obedient to his civil rulers, and was hospitable to his friends.

But as we walked to find Dives to interview him, we might only have noticed a bundle of rags near Dives's gate. The pile was called Lazarus. He did not even have enough energy to be a street person. He lay at the gate of the rich man's house, wishing for any small help—the scraps from the rich man's table. But Dives, being a responsible member of society ("waste not, want not"), appears not to have allowed leftovers to be randomly distributed to the undeserving poor. So Lazarus waited in vain.

Not even having the energy to care for himself, Lazarus was infected by sores festering on his body. The only members of Dives's household who found Lazarus interesting were the dogs, who came and licked the open sores as he lay there. Lazarus does not even seem to have known how best to exhibit his pain and distress to excite the sympathy of passers-by, who might generously have consoled him for the blow God had given him. He just lay listlessly there by the gate of Dives's clean and spacious home.

The Law of Moses is clear. The rich are obligated to aid the poor from their own abundance. According to the Law, Dives ought to have helped Lazarus. He should, if nothing else, have given aid to all the beggars who sat by his gate. But he didn't. Lazarus continued to squat silently in his poverty. The Law's judgment on Dives was deferred. Nothing happened. Or so it appeared.

Now a few years ago I went home to Dallas, on a dual-purpose journey. There I attended a conference of the American Academy of Religion, duly delivering a paper. I also went home to visit with my parents in the house in which I grew up.

The conference itself was in one of Dallas's magnificent new hotels, with large open courtyard spaces, flamboyant banners, and sleek glass and aluminum elevators. Nothing was spared to make this hotel an expression of the power of Texas oil and commercial money. The architectural lines were straight and powerful; the space was almost overwhelming. The chairs, the shops, the plants, and the escalators were new, sturdy, and overtly expensive.

The ordinary clientele of this luxuriant hotel bustled busily to and fro. They were the wheelers and dealers in high finance, oil brokers, managers and owners of new industries who have come to the Sun Belt to escape the unions and build factories with cheap labor. All wore silk, finely woven cottons, or thin woolen suits. The women's gold and silver jewelry was of the best contemporary design, and the men were discretely and elegantly clothed.

When my father picked me up at the hotel and we drove home, our old neighborhood was much as I remembered it from childhood. Some houses had been repainted and refinished. Others had declined further, with paint peeling, doors coming off hinges, and ever-expanding holes knocked in the walls. The alley was still full of ruts, the neighbor's trash still overflowed the cans, and the front lawn next door still looked like a perpetual garage sale.

A couple of blocks from our house stood the same row of rooming houses I remembered from my childhood. On the porches and the balconies still sat rank upon rank of mothers with hopeless faces, most without spouses or supportive family, watching their children, for whom they sometimes can find clothes. As always, the dull welfare diet nourishes vacant faces and limited horizons for both young and old.

So the cycle repeats itself. A few miles from the affluent hotel live households of people who are unsure if they will be able to have shoes when the ones they are wearing disintegrate, who cannot obtain a physician's help, and who cannot send their children to school without fearing that they will be gunned down in the hallway. It appeared to me that Lazarus lives in East Dallas near the fairgrounds, and Dives still eats at Antoine's, shops at Neiman-Marcus, and drives home to Highland Park.

Why is Lazarus still at the gate? Why is Dives still free to ignore Lazarus and care only for himself? Will justice be deferred until the last judgment, perhaps so that the poor can suffer more and warm the fires more intensely for the oppressive rich? Are Dives and Lazarus doomed to eternally destructive alienation from each other?

In Georges Bernanos's *The Diary of a Country Priest* the Cure de Torcy speaks to the young priest about the mystery of poverty. Out of his own experience as an activist who worked with his congregation of Flemish miners to improve their conditions, and who is now laboring as a pastor in a small French town, he struggles to express the pain of his effort to aid his own people, and of his realization that there will always be rich and poor.

"The poor you will always have with you because there will always be hard and grasping people who want power even more than possessions."[3] The poverty of those who do not have possessions, the Cure de Torcy suggests, is simply the physical image of a fundamental human illusion, to which rich and poor can be prey. Poverty is the emptiness in our hearts and in our heads. All of us share in this illusion. Some are forced to live out in their everyday lives the physical manifestation of this emptiness; others let poverty overcome their souls, so that they grab possessions for themselves and push others into a poverty that enchains the body and sometimes the soul as well.

For this reason the poor—who are more truly called those whom our society has made poor—enrage us who have power and possessions. If we truly see them, we behold the emptiness in ourselves and in all we make. We recognize that we have made the poor to feed our emptiness. Our comfortable souls wax prosperous if we behold them trapped in despair or pinching their money to aim for a comfort they can never attain. Because we can never accept them, or the emptiness in ourselves that causes them, we make the poor, asserts the Cure de Torcy, into "a dead weight which our proud civilizations will pass on to each other with fear and loathing."

But Jesus' parable suggests another ending is possible. If Dives had looked into Lazarus's face he would have been compelled to see the emptiness in his own soul, the vulnerability of his own suffering and death, the thin margin of luck keeping him in the mansion and not crippled by the gate. If Dives had gazed into Lazarus's eyes, he could no longer have continued to dress in fine linen while Lazarus suffered in dirty rags. If Dives had spoken and heard Lazarus, then he could not have continued to feast while Lazarus starved.

On the other hand, if Lazarus had looked up to Dives and spoken to him as one human being to another who had been luckier than he, then could Lazarus have fallen back into the same helplessness, the passivity that sapped from him the energy even to clean his sores? If Dives and Lazarus had ever known each other, spoken to each other, seen each other's vulnerability and emptiness, or had given to each other, then what might have resulted? But such an encounter never occurred.

Today Dives and Lazarus, rich and poor, haves and have-nots, those who have a little but need more, still live—in Dallas, New York, and in all our cities and parishes and homes. What emptiness, what bitterness, what hostility between us, what refusal to meet each other, to acknowledge the need of each to find ourselves in the other! If we remain apart, Jesus warns, judgment will come inevitably—judgment by God in the afterlife and, we add, through social dissolution and revolution in this life. Such a fate may be postponed for a time, but inevitably God's judgment expressed in violent social revolt will pull down nations and peoples.

God calls the church to declare the coming of this inexorable judgment to Dives and Lazarus today, just as Jesus did in his own time. But as Jesus did, we proclaim hope also. Through Christ's death and resurrection we are given the commission to begin to establish in this world God's reconciling love. We are invited to share together at one eucharistic table, in which God strengthens and nourishes us with one food and drink, his own life offered to us. We anticipate on earth the heavenly banquet, in which there will be neither rich nor poor, but where we will all share together in one communion with God. Lazarus, Dives, and all of us sit as equals at one table of the Lord. Here Dives and Lazarus meet and help each other. Here they are joined in Christ's communion.

Fed in hope by God, we are empowered by God's grace to share together here and now the earthly food belonging to all of us as God's children, and as sisters and brothers of one another. The good news summons us to envision a world in which rich and poor live together with each person receiving by right enough for a genuinely human life. In our homes, our parishes, and our governments, God calls us to work in every way we can to make that vision real here and now. This very day God puts judgment and hope before us. In the power of the Holy Spirit, let us go forth into the world to struggle to bring God's reign of love and justice to every part of our waiting world.

7
Preaching as Liturgical Prayer and Sacramental Act

Today basic books both about liturgy and about preaching insist that "sermons are not interruptions of the liturgy but integral parts thereof."[1] That apparently simple assertion involves an assumption that the liturgy is intended to be one unified action with different components, of which the sermon is one. Undergirding this idea is the belief that liturgy is the prayer of the Christian community.

Everything in this book is founded on the presupposition that preaching is a part of the liturgy, and as such, is liturgical prayer. The very form of preaching emerges from its place and role in the Christian community's corporate worship, which is foremost the Sunday eucharistic liturgy of word and sacrament. In previous chapters we have explored how sermons take form and shape as prayer in and for the liturgy. Now we inquire about the interconnection between the sermon as prayer focused through images and the whole liturgy of which the sermon is a part.

Our starting point is preaching as an integral part of the liturgy of the Eucharist. In *Homiletic* David Buttrick makes an old but helpful distinction between "in-church" speaking, which is "speaking to the faithful who have been baptized in Christ," and "out-church" speaking, which is addressed to those who are not within the church. He shifts the focus of the distinction from the audience (the baptized in the church and the unbaptized outside) to the place (in church, in the liturgy; and outside in day-to-day life). Buttrick envisages in-church preaching as primarily the task of the ordained persons in the church, whereas outside preaching is the witness of the laity. Because in-church preaching exists in the liturgy that feeds the community's life, in-church preaching should focus and nourish all other proclamation of the Word

95

in this world.[2] All preaching is thus rooted in the eucharistic liturgy; most of the preaching for which training is required will be situated in the liturgy itself.

The theological roots of this vision of preaching are firmly planted in the fundamental perception of prayer as an interchange between God and humanity, the image of "angels of God ascending and descending."[3] In the eucharistic liturgy the community of the baptized receives God's self-revelation and responds in grace. In the hearing of the Word, the affirmation of faith, the offering of bread and wine and self, the consecration of the elements in the power of the Holy Spirit, the reception of the eucharistic Christ, and the sending forth in the world—in the whole movement of the liturgy—God's people gather to renew and nurture their essential relationships with God. Preaching is that part of the prayer articulating the vision of redemption and transformation for this particular community in time and space.

PREACHING AS LITURGICAL PRAYER

In the structure of the Eucharist, preaching links the proclamation of the Scriptures with the table liturgy. In the Scriptures we hear the Word of God proclaimed, but in words and deeds of a past time and place. How is this biblical story our story today? How does this Scripture relate us to God and God to us? What difference does this Scripture make in our lives? How is it good news to us? The preacher's responsibility is to discern and proclaim this Scripture as God's Word to us, entering deeply into the tension and conflict in our lives between what we are and what we are called to be, and opening to us the way to transformation in God.

Analogous to the speech of daily life, the sermon provides a time when we recall the stories of our own life, our family, and our people, and when we explore the impact of the past on our present. In our family, for instance, we might have an old hoe that usually lies on a shelf in mother's study. But on a Sunday afternoon, when everyone is sitting on the front porch, someone carries out the hoe and asks: what is this? Then father tells how mother's great-great grandparents used to be slaves in southeastern Texas. But after the Civil War they moved up to eastern Texas and became sharecroppers. They worked day in and day out, earning enough to give their children clean clothes, a few books, and the courage to go to college in Georgia.

That hoe, says Dad, reminds us of their hard work, which gave this family hope that if we worked and struggled, we could do better. Mother adds her own memories of how her parents had struggled as high school teachers to help her all the way to the end of her doctoral education. The conversation then is turned by the parents, to questions about the present day: Have we lost our hope that education and work are important and will give us satisfaction? Why haven't the efforts represented by our ancestors' rusty hoe cured the terrible endemic poverty of so many in the black community? Is there anything that we blacks who are more successful can do for poorer members of the black community, or should we concentrate on protecting our own gains?

In such a discourse, one specific object—the hoe—is the focus for a key story from the past, which incorporates human values together with a vision of hope for the family's and the community's futures, and which raises questions about present and future for members of the family. In the Sunday ritual of the family's gathering together, the story nurtures in the family members strong bonds of affiliation, and an encouragement to live by family values. The sermon contains some of those same elements. It also remembers the past and connects it with our present and future. It involves the hearers in a process of recalling the past and exploring its power and meaning for here and now.

In *Christ and Sacred Speech*, Gail Ramshaw discusses the particular power and significance of liturgical language. Liturgical language, including the words of the sermon, is sacred speech, words through which God is revealed to us and we return praise to God.[4] The peculiar quality of sacred speech is its capacity to connect God and the earthly realm. Sacred speech is the language of prayer, words from and to God.

The preacher's task is to shape the sermon so that we hear God addressing us, recalling the divine words and deeds among us, which affect and shape us even today. And we, having listened and reflected, respond to God still living among us.[5] The remembering of God's past deeds and words differs from our family reminiscences, no matter how powerful, because the God whose stories we retell and respond to still lives and addresses us in the present. Our language of liturgical prayer interconnects us with God here and now, knitting God's past deeds together with our present reality. In the specific context of the eucharistic liturgy, the sermon leads us to the table, where we speak and act our response to the gift of divine life. In the sermon, this specific congregation of the baptized is incorporated into the mystery of God's transforming love as it is proclaimed in a particular facet of God's relationship with the world.

In the sermon the congregation is challenged and comforted by a reminder of its continuing relationship with the biblical God who is still today our God, and who invites us to enter more fully into the mystery of divine life and love. As we continue our liturgical prayer, we gather around the altar, where God has invited us to the banquet. By gathering around the table our community is changed, as St. Augustine wrote, by becoming what we eat. As the community's prayer continues in the eucharistic meal, we are invited to let ourselves be transformed by the grace the sermon proclaims.

The sermon connects the word and table in the liturgy, both by bringing the Scriptures alive for the congregation, and by evoking the desire for redemption and change possible only through transformation in Christ. In an effective sermon, the hearers will become a part of the world of the Scriptures, appreciating how God acts and invites them to the change in their lives that the exposure of their weakness and sin require. The sermon will move the hearers to perceive their need and hope for transformation in their own lives. Directly or indirectly, the sermon invites the congregation to be nourished for this transformation in the eucharistic meal.

On a practical level the very nature of preaching requires that sermons be prepared with acute awareness that they are part of a larger act of worship. Consequently, a sermon should never be an oration or inspiring talk with no reference or relationship to the liturgy of which it is part. Nor ought it to be simply exegesis, an intellectual exposition of some feature of the Scriptures, or hagiography. Neither the preacher nor the congregation ought to lose sight of the sermon's character as liturgical prayer through which the congregation remembers and receives God's words and deeds among them, the transforming hope for their lives, and their nourishment around the table for a continuing journey with God.

PREACHING AS SACRAMENTAL ACT

If we assume that preaching is an integral part of the eucharistic liturgy, then it follows that preaching is a sacramental act. Different preachers have spoken of the closeness of preaching to the sacraments, either as being nourished by the sacraments or as enriching people's sharing in the sacraments. These observations are true, but not strong enough. The preaching of the Word is not some reality external or accidental to the sacrament of the Lord's Supper, the Eucharist. From its beginnings the Christian community has understood preaching as integral to the eucharistic liturgy. The total eucharistic action manifests Christ's incarnation among us, inviting us to partake of his life; preaching is "an existential, incarnated application . . . a sacramental act, sharing in the sacrament of the Word."[6] As integral to one of the fundamental sacramental acts of the church, preaching is undeniably sacramental.

In what way is preaching sacramental? No one definition of sacrament satisfies everyone, but one common starting point is Augustine's description that a sacrament is a "sign of something" (*Letters* 138.1). This description contains in itself an idea of a tangible, sensory reality representing and conveying a divine reality. At the heart of all later differences of opinion rests an agreement that this sensory event with its actions, words, and objects joins the human with the divine, and nourishes the human with divine life.

The sacramental character of preaching derives from its interconnection with the entire eucharistic worship of the church. Because the sermon is part of and interdependent on the Eucharist, it shares in the sacramental character of the Eucharist. The preacher does well to remember that her or his sermon, with its words, gestures, vestments, physical position, duration in time, and so on, is one element of the entire eucharistic action. In both preparation and delivery, the preacher will be helped by remembering that the sermon is one element of the sacrament, spoken in and with the community as a part of its sacramental prayer.

This sacramental nature of preaching also encourages the preacher to speak the language of sacraments—image and story. The spoken words of the preacher, which "fall upon ears of flesh," are appropriate sacramental actions for embodied people redeemed and called by an incarnate God.[7] The sermon gives form, shape, and image to the prayerful relationship between the people and God's Word, and the transformation God offers them through the grace of the Eucharist. From that perspective, homiletic language that is concrete and image-centered is congruent with the specificity and incarnational character of all sacramental prayer.

THE INCARNATIONAL CHARACTER OF PREACHING

Incarnational is a much overused term in theological circles. None-theless, it is an appropriate characterization of preaching. Because preaching is ultimately part of the sacramental act of the Eucharist, it tries through words to picture the activity of God in the matter of this world, its time and space, and all its human and animal inhabitants. Preaching focuses its words in the concrete, the specific, and the ordinary, because the God we know through the Bible became flesh for us in Jesus Christ. God is known to us through light and darkness, mother hens and soaring eagles, and in the human face of Jesus. Good preaching is rooted in the senses, because God became known to us in the flesh.

Preaching is also, as we noted earlier in this chapter, part of liturgical activity; it incorporates in its unfolding all the senses of the human body—sight, smell, hearing, touch, taste. Cyprian Vagaggini, for instance, has formulated an elaborate definition of liturgy that rests on its sensory character: "The liturgy is the complexus of the sensible, efficacious, signs of the Church's sanctification and of her worship."[8] At the center of liturgy is its relationship to the reality that gives rise to the mystery of Christian life and community: the incarnation of the Word made flesh. In its own limited way, preaching continues this incarnational activity, rooted in the Eucharist action.

In the Eucharist, the Christian community gathers together, in all its fallible enfleshment, to hear its story and to share a meal through which God nourishes us in the divine life and joins us more closely to believers throughout the ages. The whole eucharistic drama is an action of bodies in time and space with an incarnate Word who makes our story God's own. In such a liturgy, preaching that remains centered in images and in the story of Israel and of the church keeps us in touch with the incarnate, tangible, fleshly character of the human encounter with God.[9]

Through such imagery-centered preaching, we come to know a God whose words and deeds encounter a feeling, thinking, sensing humanity. Preaching focused in imagery also reminds us that the God who became flesh meets us and redeems us in our embodied reality—sight and sound, head and heart, body and soul.

In praying the liturgy with the congregation, the preacher needs to be sensitive to the character of the liturgy as a sensory reality in which

God is active and present. The sensory quality of liturgy includes architecture, the vestments and hangings, the furnishings, any paintings or statuary, the interior design of the church, the places where people stand and sit, the interplay of movements of all the participants in the liturgy, the music, the spoken and sung words of the liturgy, and the imagery they create and invoke. If the preacher is attentive to the interplay of the sensory reality of the liturgy, the sermon can most prayerfully and helpfully express the ascending and descending of the angels in that community of God's people gathered together in Christ.

CONCLUSION

As we grow in our efforts to develop an image-filled approach to preaching, we will find our sermons addressing more effectively the whole human being, body and soul, heart and head. Our purpose in so doing is to bring each of us close to God and to one another. Images appeal to the many dimensions of the human person—intellect, heart, and body—anchoring us in one reality through which God is revealed and acts in the whole self.

The image provides a focus, the place of encounter between God and the human hearer. The preacher's task is to provide, within the context of the liturgy, the most moving and carefully wrought images possible to allow that encounter to take place. In *On Christian Doctrine*, in which he sets down some of his own thoughts on preaching, Augustine of Hippo writes about his experience of preaching about the simple image of the cup of cold water given in Jesus' name:

> Is it not the case that when we happen to speak on this subject to the people, and the presence of God is with us . . . a tongue of fire springs out of the cold water which inflames even cold human hearts with a zeal for doing good in hope of eternal life? (IV.18.37)

The preacher's vocation is to preach so that flames of fire leap out of the images of cups of cold water, and from all those images proclaimed in the sermons of our liturgy. In pervious chapters of this book, we have explored the cultural and theological roots of our need for images in preaching, examined the connections between preaching and prayer, and discussed specific ways of prayer that help one prepare one's sermons. We have concluded with considerations of preaching as liturgical prayer, and the relationship of preaching to the rest of the liturgy. My hope is that through prayerful sermons, shaped by biblical image and story, God's grace will enkindle in human hearts the flaming zeal by which we see God in the world, and by which we share with others what we have been given.

Notes

INTRODUCTION

1. Humbert of Romans, "Treatise on the Formation of Preachers," *Early Dominicans: Selected Writings*, ed. Simon Tugwell (New York: Paulist Press, 1982), 184-85.

2. See "plot," *A Dictionary of Literary, Dramatic, and Cinematic Terms*, ed. Sylvan Barnet, Morton Berman, William Burto (Boston: Little, Brown, and Company, 1960, 1971) 83-86.

3. See "imagery," ibid., 61.

4. Margaret R. Miles, *Image as Insight* (Boston: Beacon Press, 1985), 10-12, 35-39.

5. John Booty, *The Christ We Know* (Boston: Cowley Press, 1987), 47.

6. For some contemporary definitions of preaching, see David Buttrick, *Homiletic: Moves and Structures* (Philadelphia: Fortress, 1987), 11-13; Fred B. Craddock, *Preaching* (Nashville: Abingdon Press, 1985), 17; O. C. Edwards, *Elements of Homiletic* (New York: Pueblo Publication, 1982), 7. In *The Christ We Know*, 71-76, Booty refers to the understanding of preaching as prayer in the Anglican tradition.

1. IMAGERY AND THE MIND

1. Ernest Cassirer, *The Philosophy of Symbolic Forms*, 3 vols. (New Haven, Conn.: Yale University Press, 1953); Susan Langer, *Philosophy in a New Key* (New York: New American Library, 1942, 1951).

2. *A Dictionary of Literary, Dramatic, and Cinematic Terms*, 61.

3. Miles, *Image as Insight*, 35.

4. *Preaching Biblically*, ed. Don M. Wardlaw (Philadelphia: Westminster Press, 1983), contains an excellent introduction to some of these issues in the context of biblical preaching. Eugene Lowrie's *The Homiletical Plot* (Atlanta: John Knox Press, 1980) and Henry Mitchell's *The Recovery of Preaching* (New York: Harper & Row, 1977) address the question primarily in terms of story and narrative preaching. Thomas Troeger's *Creating Fresh Images for Preaching* (Valley Forge, Pa.: Judson Press, 1982) directly addresses the issues of imagery.

5. John Gay's *Freud: A Mind for Our Times* (New York: W. W. Norton, 1988) offers a substantial study of Freud's theories and influence. Charles Hampden-Turner's *Maps of the Mind* (New York: Macmillan, 1981) offers an overview of Freudian and other ancient and modern psychological theories (40-71). Although each sketch is brief, the author offers an incisive "atlas of the mind" for graphic and convenient comparison.

6. Recently, much has been written about scientific discoveries about the brain and thought. Hampden-Turner, *Maps of the Mind* (72-97), contains some of the major paradigms. Anthony Smith, *The Mind* (New York: Viking, 1984), offers a good overview of contemporary scientific understanding of the brain and its functions. Judith Hooper and Dick Teresi's *The Three Pound Universe* (New York: Macmillian, 1986) sketches the biology of the mind, various states of consciousness, and the relationship between brain and mind.

7. Two basic books on the question of moral development are: Lawrence Kohlberg, *The Philosophy of Moral Development* (San Francisco: Harper & Row, 1981), and Carol Gilligan, *In a Different Voice* (Cambridge: Harvard University Press, 1982).

8. For an overview of these questions, see Thomas Kuhn, *The Essential Tension* (Chicago: University of Chicago Press, 1977) and *The Structure of Scientific Revolutions* (Chicago: University of Chicago Press, 1970). Frijof Capra, in *The Tao of Physics* (New York: Random House, 1975), explores the intersection of imaginative insight and scientific method in modern physics.

9. In *The Primal Mind: Vision and Reality in Indian America* (New York: Harper & Row, 1981) is a comprehensive, sensitive treatment of two world views appreciative of strengths and weakness in differing visions. In *The Sacred Hoop* (Boston: Beacon Press, 1986) Paula Gunn Allen attempts to recover the feminine in Native American traditional vision.

10. Highwater, *The Primal Mind*, 75.

11. Mircea Eliade's *Cosmos and History* (New York: Harper & Row, 1959) explores differing notions of time and history.

12. One of the clearest and most precise introductions to liberation theology is Justo and Catherine Gonzalez's *Liberation Preaching* (Nashville: Abingdon Press, 1980). Deane William Ferm's two-volume set *Third World Liberation Theologies: An Introductory Survey* and *Third World Liberation Theologies: A Reader* (Maryknoll, N.Y.: Orbis Books, 1986) offers a more comprehensive introduction.

13. For an introduction, *Women Spirit Rising*, ed. C. Christ and J. Plaskow (San Francisco: Harper & Row, 1979), is an essential sourcebook. A more recent, although not so comprehensive, introduction is *Christian Feminism: Visions of a New Humanity*, ed. Judith Weidman (San Francisco: Harper & Row, 1984). Margaret Miles presents an avidly feminist epistemology in connection with women's place in the religious community in *Image as Insight*. Barbara J. MacHaffie, *Her Story: Women in Christian Tradition* (Philadelphia: Fortress Press, 1986), offers an overview of women in Christian history and thought. Patricia Wilson-Kastner, *Faith, Feminism, and the Christ* (Philadelphia: Fortress Press, 1983), presents an overview of different Christian feminists, as well as a constructive perspective. Rosemary Radford Ruether, *Sexism*

and Godtalk (Boston: Beacon Press, 1983), offers a broad systematic feminist theological perspective. Sallie McFague, *Models of God* (Philadelphia: Fortress Press, 1987), continues her pioneering work in feminist theology in a global perspective.

2. BIBLICAL IMAGERY

1. Standard references such as the *Interpreter's Dictionary of the Bible* are most helpful. Othmar Keel's *The Symbolism of the Biblical World* (New York: Seabury Press, 1978) is useful. Overviews such as *The World of the Bible*, ed. A. S. van der Woude (Grand Rapids, Mich.: Wm. B. Eerdmans, 1986), and collections of primary texts such as *The Ancient Near East*, ed. James B. Prichard, vol. 1 & 2 (Princeton, N.J.: Princeton Univ. Press, 1958, 1975), can give essential background, pictures, and documents about and from ancient Near Easterners.

2. Nick Herbert, *Quantum Reality* (Garden City, N.Y.: Anchor/Doubleday, 1985), 250.

3. In addition to the works cited in 1 above, the preacher will find a concordance (such as *Strong's Exhaustive Concordance of the Bible* [Nashville: Abingdon Press, 1890, 1980]) indispensable. Also essential are good translations with extensive notes and cross references, such as *New Oxford Annotated Bible with the Apocrypha*, ed. Herbert G. May and Bruce M. Metzger (New York: Oxford University Press, 1977) or *The New Jerusalem Bible* (Garden City, N.Y.: Doubleday and Co., 1985). The preacher will also want to consult such thematic studies as Thierry Maertens' *Bible Themes—A Source Book* (Bruges: Biblica, 1964) and Gerhard Kittel's *Theological Dictionary of the New Testament* (Grand Rapids, Mich.: Wm. B. Eerdmans, 1964–1976). Another is *The Westminster Dictionary of Christian Theology*, ed. Alan Richardson and John Bowden (Philadelphia: Westminster Press, 1983).

4. *The Symbolism of the Biblical World*, 179-83.

5. Ibid., 195; Phyllis Trible, *God and the Rhetoric of Sexuality* (Philadelphia: Fortress, 1978), 33-34.

6. Bernard Lonergan, *Insight* (New York: Philosophical Library, 1957, 1961), treats both the human urge to question (p.9) and the relation between symbolism and questioning (pp. 17-19). My vocabulary and perspective are not the same as Lonergan's, but I am indebted to him for his perceptions of the importance of imagery and symbolism in the context of human understanding.

7. Claude Tresmontant, *La Métaphysique du Christianisme et la naissance de la philosophie chrétienne* (Paris: Editions de Seuil, 1961); D. S. Wallace-Hadrill, *The Greek Patristic View of Nature* (New York: Barnes and Noble, 1968); Matthew Fox, *Original Blessing* (Santa Fe, N.M.: Bear and Co., 1983).

8. C. H. Dodd's classic study *The Parables of the Kingdom* (London: Religious Book Club, 1935, 1942) remains fundamental. Two important studies about biblical imagery are Sally McFague's *Metaphorical Theology: Models of God in Religious Imagery* (Philadelphia: Fortress Press, 1982) and C. B. Caird, *The Language and Imagery of the Bible* (Philadelphia: Westminster, 1980).

9. Bernard Brandon Scott, *The Word of God in Words: Reading and Preaching the Gospels* (Philadelphia: Fortress Press, 1985).

3. PREACHING THE IMAGE:
HOW CAN THE WORDS WORK?

1. Edward F. Markquart, *Quest for Better Preaching* (Minneapolis: Augsburg, 1985), 131-175, offers a summary of some of these developments. Some significant individual works are: Henry G. Davis, *Design for Preaching* (Philadelphia: Fortress Press, 1958); Eugene Lowrie, *The Homiletical Plot* (Atlanta: John Knox Press, 1980); Wesley A. Kort, *Narrative Elements and Religious Meaning* (Philadelphia: Fortress Press, 1975); Edmund A. Steimle, Morris J. Neidenthal, and Charles L. Rice, *Preaching the Story* (Philadelphia: Fortress Press, 1980). Bruce C. Salmon, *Storytelling in Preaching* (Nashville: Broadman Press, 1988), offers theoretical and practical guidance in the use of story and imagery in preaching, with an extended annotated bibliography, 135-152.

2. John R. Donahue, *The Gospel in Parable: Metaphor, Narrative, and Theology in the Synoptic Gospel* (Philadelphia: Fortress Press, 1988), esp. 1-27, offers a helpful discussion of the nature of parable as imagery in story that links for the hearer this world and God's activity. On p. 21 Donahue offers a list of narrative characteristics bearing some relationship to what one might more broadly say about images in preaching.

3. G. B. Caird, *The Language and Imagery of the Bible* (Philadelphia: Westminster Press, 1980), 144-145.

4. C. H. Dodd, *The Parables of the Kingdom* (London: Religious Book Club, 1942), 16. John R. Donahue, in *The Gospel in Parable*, uses Dodd's description and elaborates it, 13-15.

5. Frederick Houk Borsch, *Many Things in Parables: Extravagant Stories of New Community* (Philadelphia: Fortress Press, 1988), 5; Bernard Lonergan, *Insight*, 531-34.

6. Cyril E. Pockne, *Cross and Crucifix* (London: Mowbrays, 1962); Frederick van der Meer and Christian Mohrmann, *Atlas of the Early Christian World* (New York: Nelson, 1958), 141-145.

7. Donahue, *The Gospel in Parable*, 17-20; Frederick Borsch, *Many Things in Parables*, 5.

8. Sallie McFague, *Metaphorical Theology* (Philadelphia: Fortress Press, 1982). She explores the theological dimensions of the metaphor of God as friend (182-92). See also her *Models of God* (Philadelphia: Fortress Press, 1987) for a discussion of the relationship of images to models (91-95), as well as chapters about God as mother, lover, and friend.

4. PRAYER: THE PREACHER'S BREAD

1. *The Poems of George Herbert*, intro. Helen Gardner (London: Oxford University Press, 1961), 44.

2. Thomas Merton, *Bread in the Wilderness* (Philadelphia: Fortress Press; Collegeville, Minn.: Liturgical Press, 1986), 8.

3. In *True Prayer: An Introduction to Christian Spirituality* (London: Sheldon Press, 1980), Kenneth Leech provides a good introduction to central classic Christian understandings of prayer; Chester Michael and Marie Norrisey, in *Prayer and Temperament* (Charlottesville, Va.: The Open Door, 1984), offers some interesting suggestions about the way temperament shapes different forms of prayer.

4. Elizabeth Canham, *Praying the Bible* (Cambridge, Mass.: Cowley Press, 1987), esp. 1-12.

5. Henry Mitchell, *The Recovery of Preaching* (San Francisco: Harper and Row, 1977) 37.

6. In *Praying the Bible*, Canham suggests some ways of using this approach, 29-46.

7. John Booty, *The Christ We Know*, 71-83; A. G. Dickens, *The Counter Reformation* (New York: Harcourt, Brace, and World, 1969), 185-188; Louis Bouyer, *Orthodox Spirituality and Protestant and Anglican Spirituality*. Vol. III of *A History of Christian Spirituality* (Minneapolis: Seabury/Winston, 1969), 133-115, 154-159; John R. H. Moorman, *The Anglican Spiritual Tradition* (Springfield, Ill.: Templegate, 1983), 65-69.

8. Urban T. Holmes, *A History of Christian Spirituality* (New York: Seabury Press, 1980), 93-5, points to some of the elements of this heritage.

9. New versions of Ignatius's *Exercises* have appeared: David Fleming, *The Spiritual Exercise of St. Ignatius: A Literal Translation and a Contemporary Reading* (St. Louis: Institute of Jesuit Sources, 1978); David Fleming, *Modern Spiritual Exercises* (Garden City, N.Y.: Doubleday/Image, 1978; David Stanley, *A Modern Scriptural Approach to the Spiritual Exercises* (Chicago: Institute of Jesuit Sources, 1967). *The Autobiography of St. Ignatius Loyola*, ed. Joseph O'Callaghan, trans. John Olin (San Francisco: Harper and Row, 1974), recounts Ignatius's own story of his conversion and growth in Christ; the preacher will note the importance of the visual, sensory dimension of Ignatius's own experience with God. A scholarly study of centrality of imagination in Ignatius's world view is provided in Antonio T. de Nicolas' *Powers of Imagining* (Albany: State University of New York, 1986). Jonathan Spence's *The Memory Palace of Matteo Ricci* (New York: Penguin Books, 1984) offers a good contemporary re-creation of the way in which Ignatius's use of imagination shaped an intellectual approach that used the visual sensory aspect of mind as the organizing and integrating locus for all human mental activity.

10. Lewis Delmage, *The Spiritual Exercise of Saint Ignatius of Loyola* (Boston: St. Paul Editions, 1978), also presents the "Three Modes of Prayer," 238-260, and "Norms for Seeking and Following the Will of God by Discriminating Between Good and Evil Influences," 313-336. Most of my discussion of the Ignatian method comes from the first week, first exercise, 41-45.

5. SHAPING THE SERMON

1. DeWitte T. Holland, *The Preaching Tradition: A Brief History* (Nashville: Abingdon, 1980); Yngve T. Brilioth, *Landmarks in the History of Preaching* (Philadelphia: Fortress Press, 1950). Edward F. Markquart, *Quest for Better*

Preaching (Minneapolis: Augsburg, 1985) 19-47. Most of the criticisms of contemporary preaching revolve around the issue of overabundant abstraction and the dominance of logic over affect.

2. Eugene Lowrie, *The Homiletical Plot* (Atlanta: John Knox Press, 1980), 22-25.

3. Despite all the modification modern critical theory and psychological theory lead one to make, John Calvin's discussion of the Holy Spirit active in the Scriptures provides an indispensible starting point. See *Institutes of the Christian Religion*, ed., J. McNeill, trans. F. L. Battles (Philadelphia: Westminster Press, 1960), I. vii. 4-5.

6. PREACHING ON THE
RICH MAN AND LAZARUS

1. Margaret Miles, *Image as Insight*, 3.

2. John R. Donahue, *The Gospel in Parable*, 162, esp. 169–72.

3. Georges Bernanos, *The Diary of a Country Priest*, trans. Pamela Morris (Garden City, N.Y.: Doubleday/Image Books, 1954, 1974), 48-49.

7. PREACHING AS LITURGICAL
PRAYER AND SACRAMENTAL ACT

1. Leonel L. Mitchell, *Praying Shapes Believing* (Minneapolis: Winston Press, 1985), 136; David Buttrick, *Homiletic* (Philadelphia: Fortress Press, 1987), 230-32, makes essentially the same point about the relationship between what he terms "in-church" preaching and the Eucharist. Dom Gregory Dix, *The Shape of the Liturgy* (London: Dacre Press, 1945, 1975), 40, 472, 596, identifies preaching as proclaiming the gospel in the liturgy, and as interpreting salvation to the congregation. Geoffrey Wainwright, "Preaching as Worship," in *The Greek Orthodox Theological Review* 28/4 (1983): 325-36, reprinted in Richard Fischer, *Theories of Preaching* (Durham, N.C.: Labyrinth Press, 1987), 353-63, outlines a classical theological vision of preaching as an element of liturgy.

2. Buttrick, *Homiletic*, 225-29.

3. Reginald Fuller, *What Is Liturgical Preaching?* (London: SCM Press, 1957), 9. In his *Theological Dimensions of the Liturgy* (Collegeville, Minn.: Liturgical Press, 1976), Cyprian Vagaggini outlines the elements of preaching and liturgical prayer that are fundamental and common (880-83). Vagaggini roots liturgy in the preaching of the Word; I think it unwise to separate word and table, historically or theologically.

4. Gail Ramshaw, *Christ in Sacred Speech: The Meaning of Liturgical Language* (Philadelphia: Fortress Press, 1986), 11-17.

5. Fuller, *What Is Liturgical Preaching?*, 22-23.

6. Gabriel M. Braso, *Liturgy and Spirituality* (Collegeville: Liturgical Press, 1971), 254. Fuller, makes helpful observations about the historical and theological unity of the liturgy of word and table. (See also Fuller, *What Is Liturgical Preaching?*, 18-22.)

7. Vagaggini explores this sacramental quality of preaching in *Theological Dimensions of the Liturgy*, 860-861.

8. Ibid., 27.

9. Ibid., 876-87.